500 FULL-SIZE PATCHWORK PATTERNS

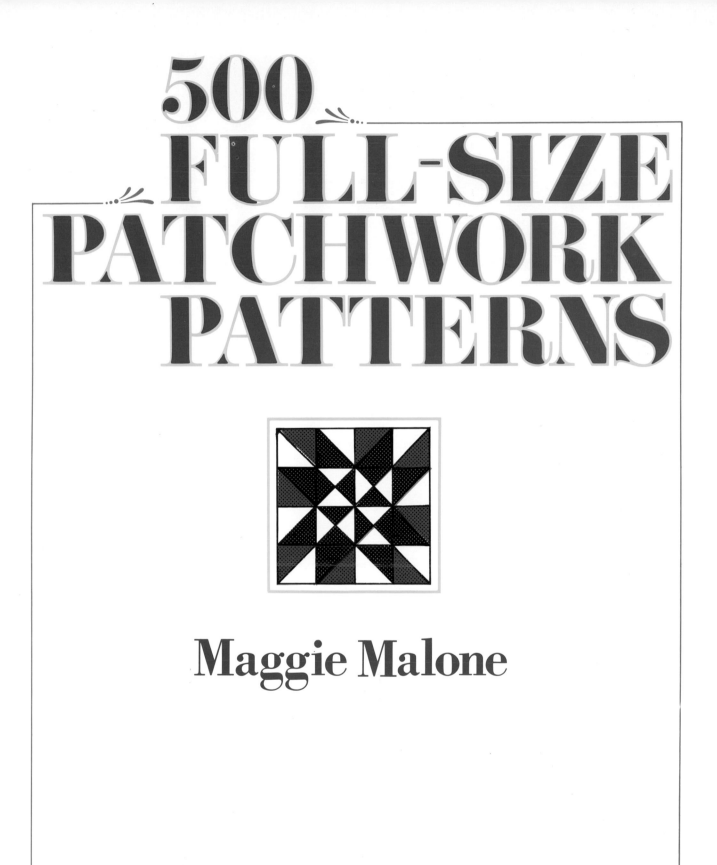

Maggie Malone

Sterling Publishing Co., Inc.   New York

Edited and designed by Barbara Busch

Library of Congress Cataloging in Publication Data

Malone, Maggie, 1942–
    500 full-size patchwork patterns.

    Includes index.
    1. Patchwork—Patterns. I. Title.
TT835.M3466   1985   746.9′7041   85-9906
ISBN 0-8069-5724-7
ISBN 0-8069-6230-5 (pbk.)

Copyright © 1985 by Sterling Publishing Co., Inc.
387 Park Avenue South, New York, N.Y. 10016
Distributed in Canada by Sterling Publishing
% Canadian Manda Group, P.O. Box 920, Station U
Toronto, Ontario, Canada M8Z 5P9
Distributed in Great Britain and Europe by Cassell PLC
Artillery House, Artillery Row, London SW1P 1RT, England
Distributed in Australia by Capricorn Ltd.
P.O. Box 665, Lane Cove, NSW 2066
Manufactured in the United States of America
All rights reserved

Contents

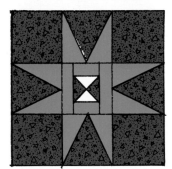

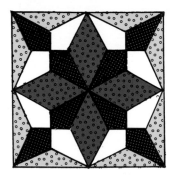

Foreword

If you liked *1001 Patchwork Designs*, you should enjoy this collection even more. The 500 designs provided are shown in the same format used in *1001 Patchwork Designs*, but with the added bonus of full-sized patterns for each and every one of them.

Some of the patterns may be familiar (although I've tried not to repeat any that have appeared in my other books), but most should be new to you.

Each time I finish a book I swear that I'm never going to look at another quilt pattern. This resolution lasts all of maybe two days, and again I'm searching for new patterns to add to my collection. I stumbled upon a bonanza when I ordered some booklets of reprints from *Hearth & Home, Nancy Page* and the *Kansas City Star. Hearth & Home* and *Nancy Page* patterns were printed in the early 1900's. The *Kansas City Star* patterns ran from 1928 to the 1960's. Many of the designs in the *Kansas City Star* had been previously published in the two sources mentioned, but I've also included many original designs from readers. I also combed antiques magazines for pictures of quilts. Many of these were original designs or unusual variations of a standard pattern. Following in the footsteps of this old tradition, some of the patterns are my own designs.

At the top of each page is given the block size. Since the blocks are standard for each section, they can be combined easily to create new designs or to make sampler quilts. I have also provided some borders.

On the next few pages are shown examples of some of the types of arrangements you can make. To me, the setting of the top has always been one of the most exciting parts of the quilting process. Certainly, it plays as vital a role as fabric selection in making each quilt individual.

The pattern is 324. Rosepoint, shown in two settings and in the process taking on two different appearances. In the top illustration, it is set diagonally and solid. In the bottom illustration, the blocks are alternated with blocks of plain fabric.

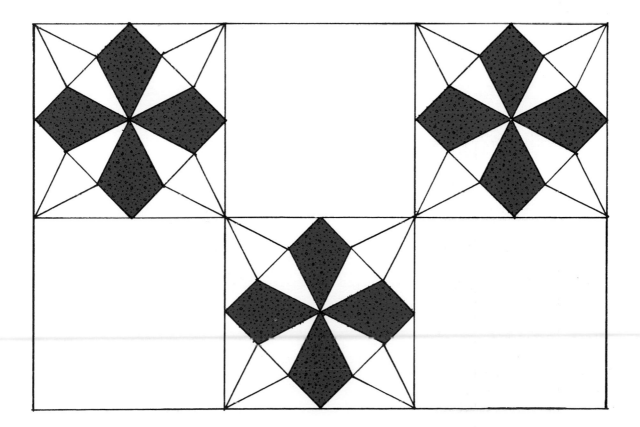

In this quilt, two blocks—342. Winged 9-Patch and 347. 9-Patch Variations are combined to produce an interesting effect.

Top row from left to right; 319. Star of the Milky Way, 193. Star of the West, 323. Poisettia. Second row. 200. Fox and Goose, 280. Green Mountain Star, 204. Lucky Pieces. Third row: 205. Aunt Nancy's Favorite, 202. Road to Damascus, 259. Wheel of Time. Bottom row: 194. Winged Square, Variation, 322. Pinwheel. The border is 498. Pinwheel. This traditional sampler uses a lattice of plain strips.

256. Chalice is not a modern design, but with this strip setting, it appears almost startlingly so.

How to Use This Book

The basic idea behind this book is that quilt patterns consist largely of geometric pieces; it is the different sizes of those pieces and their arrangements that give patchwork its tremendous variety.

Starting on page 79 are to be found the pattern pieces (in all the required sizes) that you will need to make any of the 500 designs shown in the book. If, for example, you wished to make No. 36, Box, you would look at the accompanying numbers: 3, 13, 44. You would then turn to page 81 and trace the number 3 square, following the same procedure for numbers 13 and 44. You would then treat it as any other quilt pattern.

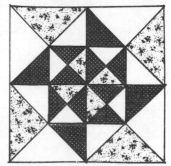

The designs are grouped by the number of patches in a block. Nine-patch blocks come first, along with their various divisions. A nine-patch block is divided into three equal squares, which can then be divided into two or three squares, making a six-patch or eighteen-patch block. Most of the designs show each square, but some of them are obscured by the shading.

Four-patch patterns come next. These include eight and twelve squares to the block. Then come the five- and seven-patch patterns.

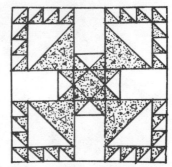

If you are at all confused by the pattern pieces and how they go together, break the block down into how many small squares make up each section. Find the pattern pieces for that design and trace them onto a large sheet of paper to the finished size given. In fact, it would be a good idea to draw the pattern out before you begin to make sure you have the proper pieces.

It will also be helpful if you know how I draft a pattern. Although it may mean more pieces per block, I try to break the block down into as many straight pieces as possible, which will usually result in all straight-seam sewing. For example, Salem, #27, was simplified by using all triangles for the center sections instead of setting a triangle into two diamonds.

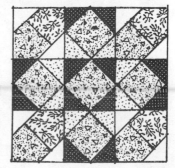

I have also found it difficult to sew two bias edges of varying sizes together. Storm at Sea, although a favorite pattern of mine, gives me fits because the long triangles don't match up in a straight line when sewn to the diamond pieces. Storm at Sea I can't do much about except struggle along, but a pattern like Linoleum #19, I can. The corner squares have been divided into four smaller squares. In this way, you are sewing two triangles together, which is pretty easy, and then sewing these to a square. You will have perfect squares every time rather than pieces sticking out on each end of the seam line. Be sure to add seam allowances to your pattern pieces.

Due to space limitations, there are a few instances where you will have to draft a pattern. If the design requires a 12-inch triangle, measure a line 12 inches across the paper, then at the end of the line, draw another line 12 inches down. Connect the ends of each line to form the triangle.

Sunshine, #372, shows a square set on end. In the center it says, 10″. To draft this pattern, draw a square 10 inches to a side. Find the middle point of each side and connect each point with a line. You now have the proper size square for the center.

A few of the patterns have pieces that belong exclusively to them. Whenever this is the case, the page number where these pieces are located will be given.

Now, look through these patterns and choose one for your next quilt. With *500 Full Size Patchwork Patterns* at your fingertips, I wish you many hours of happy quilting.

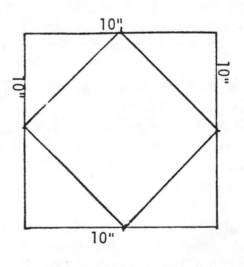

Author's Note: While putting this book together, I continued the process of simplification and found that I could eliminate some of the pattern pieces I had originally planned. For this reason, although all of the patterns are complete, certain numbers are sequentially missing.

THE BLOCKS

12-inch Blocks

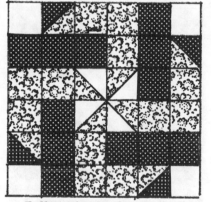

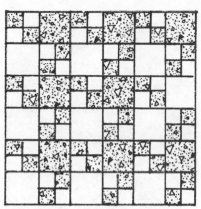

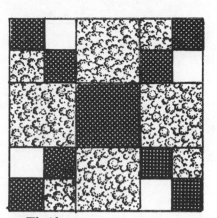

1. Carrie Nation
#1, 3

2. Cogwheel
#1, 3

3. Thrifty
#3, 5

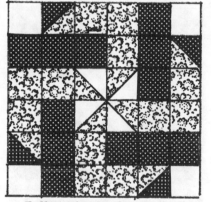

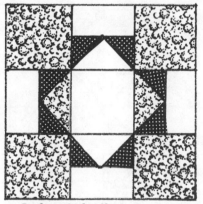

4. Follow the Leader
#3, 13, 44, 45

5. Ladies Aid Album
#5, 13, 24, 44

6. Owl
#3, 13, 24, M

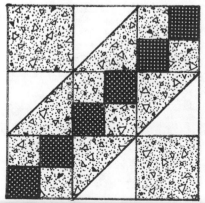

7. Road to the White House
#3, 5, 17

8. Swastika
#1, 4, 43, 45, 48

9. Interlocked Squares
#46

12-inch Blocks

10. Chained 9-Patch
#3, 5, 13, 24

11. Whirlpool
#3, 17, 24, 44

12. Dublin Steps
#3, 5, 13, 17

13. Joyce's Mystery Block
#3, 13, 17, 39

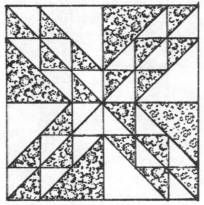

14. Mosaic I
#13, 17

15. Danger Signals
#11, 18

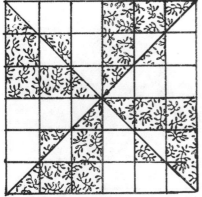

16. Betty's Delight
#3, 13

17. Kansas Star
#13, 34

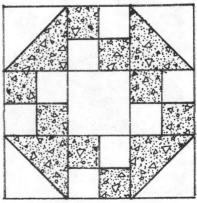

18. True Blue
#3, 5, 17

12-inch Blocks

19. Linoleum
#3, 5, 13, 44

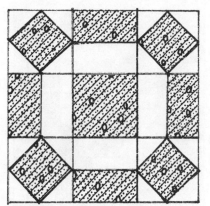

20. Squirrel in a Cage
#5, 13, 34, 44

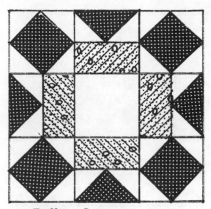

21. Rolling Squares
#5, 13, 24, 34, 44

22. Prairie Flower
#3, 5, 13, 24, 44

23. Morning Patch
#5, 13, 24, 44, B, L-1

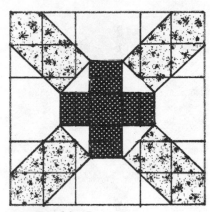

24. Double Cross I
#3, 13, 22, M

25. St. Paul
#3, 13, 24, 34, A, N

26. Ladies Aid
#13, 19, 24, 34

27. Salem
#13, 24, 34

12-inch Blocks

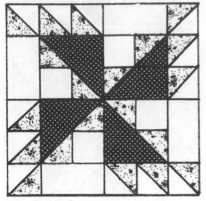

28. Strawflowers
#3, 13, 17, 44

29. Pudding and Pie
#3, 13

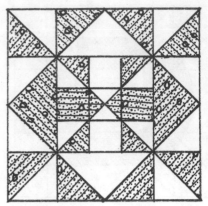

30. Belle of West Virginia
#3, 13, 15, 22, 26

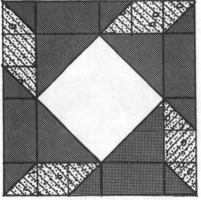

31. Turkish Puzzle
#3, 13, 17, 39, 44

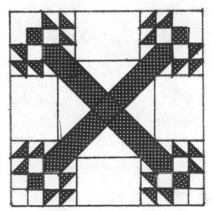

32. Queen's Crown
#1, 11, 24, 32, 48, L-3

33. Solitaire
#15, 23

34. Hovering Hawks
#5, 13, 17

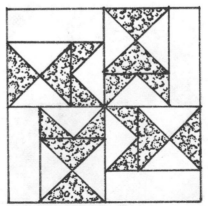

35. Flying Dutchman
#13, 24, 45

36. Box
#3, 13, 44

12-inch Blocks

37. Jewel I
#3, A-1, C-3, B-1

38. Her Sparkling Jewels
#3, 34, A-3, C-2, B-1

39. Pinwheel I
#5, 15, A-4, D-2, E, F, N-1

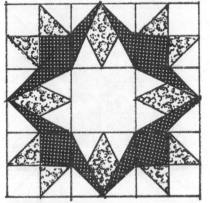

40. Starry Sky
#3, 5, 13, A-5, C-4, G

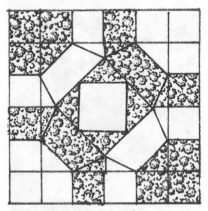

41. Oklahoma Wonder
#3, 4, 13, 23, B, N-2

42. Builder's Block
#5, 17, C-5

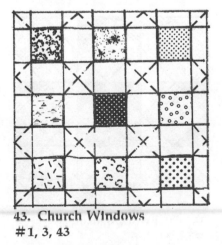

43. Church Windows
#1, 3, 43

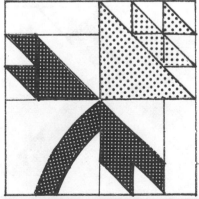

44. Windblown Lily
#7, 13, 17, 19
2" bias strip for stem, #45

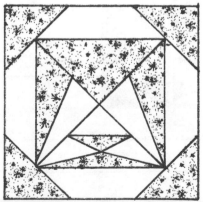

45. Mystic Emblem
#17, 24, 28, D-3, D-4, E-3, F-1, F-2, G

46. St. Gregory's Cross
#5, 13, 24, 34

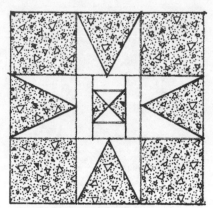

47. Dove at the Window
#5, 22, 41, 43, A-1, B-1

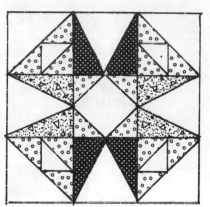

48. Maltese Star
#13, 17, 34, A-1, B-1

49. Augusta
#13, 24, 34, A, F-10

50. Bright Side
#24, 32, 34, A-6, F-4

51. Pathfinder
#3, 13, 32, see page 146

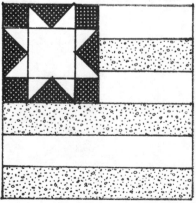

52. New York
#2, 4, 12, 23, 45, 2″ x 12″ strip

53. The Cross
#13, 24, 2¾″ square,
2¾″ x 14¼″ strip (see page 143)

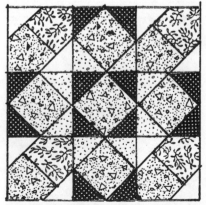

54. Patchwork Bedspread
#13, 34, L-6

12-inch Blocks

55. Royal Star I
#3, A-7, C-6, F-5, K

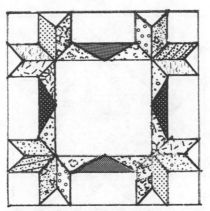

56. Chicken Foot
#3, 7, 22, 44, C-7, D-5, F-6

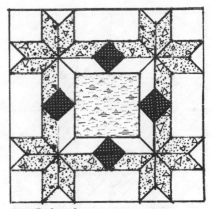

57. Golgotha
#3, 5, 22, 32, 44, C-7

58. Historic Oak Leaf
#5, 7, 13, 17, 19, bias tape
for stem

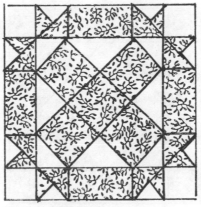

59. Easy Ways
#3, 13, 22, 24, 34, 44

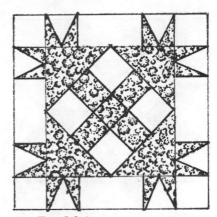

60. Des Moines
#3, 17, 32, 33, 44, A-5, B, L-7

61. Lost Ship
#22, A-8, B, B-2

62. Cabin Windows
#1, 15, 32, 35, L-8

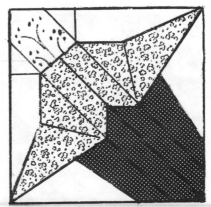

63. Trumpet Flower I
#13, 49, B-3, D, D-1, D-6, E-4,
L-9, L-10, L-11

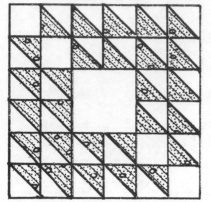

64. Indian Plume (diagonal set w/alternate plain)
#3, 5, 13

65. King's Crown
#3, 13, 17, 24, 39

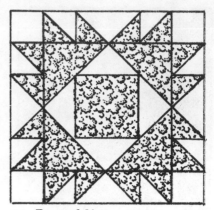

66. Framed X
#3, 5, 13, 17, 24

67. Friendship Block
#3, 13, 24, 34, L-9

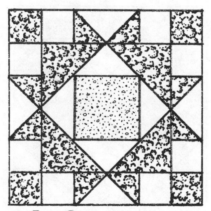

68. Four Crowns
#3, 5, 13, 17, 24

69. Chinese Block
#3, 5, 13, 17, 24, 44

70. Diamond Star
#13, 34, C-8

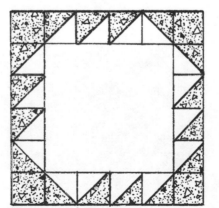

71. Dove of Peace
#3, 17, 8″ square (a dove is quilted in the center)

72. Autumn Maze
#13, 17, 24

12-inch Blocks

73. Cedars of Lebanon
#3, 13, 17, 44

74. Flying Cross
#1, 5, 11, 17

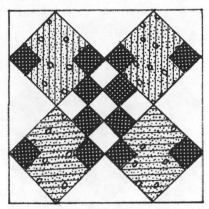

75. Eva's Delight
#15, 26, 32, M-3

76. Double L
#45, see page 147

77. Centennial Tree
#3, 13, 17, 44, L-12, see
page 147

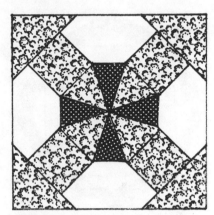

78. Harvest Home
#17, 34, A, A-9, N-3

79. Happy New Year I
#3, 13, A-5, F-6

80. Jack's Delight
#17, 24, 39

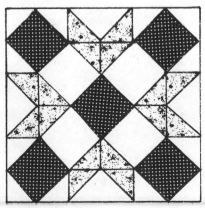

81. Joy Bells
#3, 24, 34

82. Housewife I
#3, 13, 17, 24

83. Firecrackers and Rockets
#13, A-1, A-5, A-13, B-4, F-6, D-7, K-1

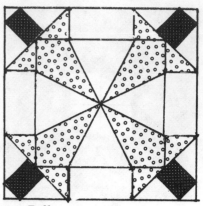

84. Bells
#11, 13, 44, A-1, 23, K-1, L-13

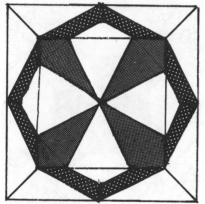

85. Bull's-Eye
#A-1, D-10, F-7, G-2, K-1

86. Blue Skies
#39, A-10, A-11, D-9, E-5

87. Noon and Night
#3, 13, 24, 17, E-4

88. New Mexico
#3, 13, 22, 24, 34, 44

89. Treasure Box
#13, 17, 24, 34

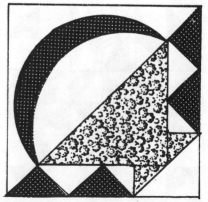

90. Basket Patch
#13, 17, 24, 8″ and 12″ triangles, see page 155

91. Happy Hunting Grounds
#5, 13, 28, A-3, G-3

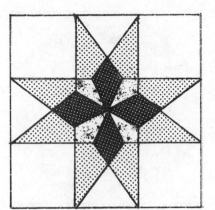

92. Wishing Star
#5, 22, A-5, A-7, D-11, K-2

93. Strawflower
#13, 22, 32, 49, A-5, A-14, B, K

94. Christmas Star I
#3, 5, 13, 22, 24, L-14, L-15

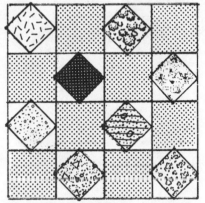

95. Four-Patch Scrap
#4, 33

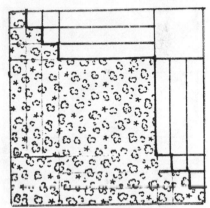

96. Hill and Valley (alternate two prints) #1, 4, 7, 46

97. Floral Centerpiece (13″)
#4, 15, 33, 23, #1, 1″ x 12″ strip

98. Vortex
#13, 17, 24, 34, C-8

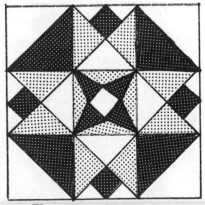

99. Phoenix
#17, 22, 24, 32, A-15, F-6

12-inch Blocks

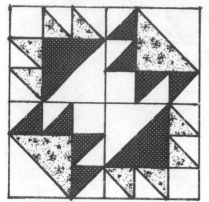

100. Tangled Briars
#3, 13, 17

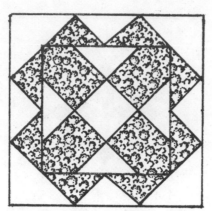

101. Four T's
#17, 24, 34, L-9

102. Bright Hopes
#3, 44

103. Montgomery
#5, 15, 17, 22, L-17

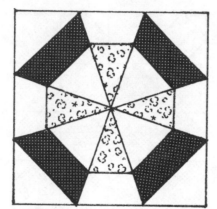

104. Denver
#17, A-12, A-16, E-7, E-8

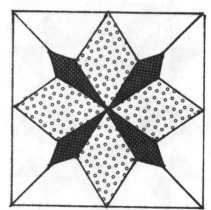

105. Oriental Star
#C-9, D-11, K-3

106. Danish Star
#3, 5, 11, 13, 22, 32

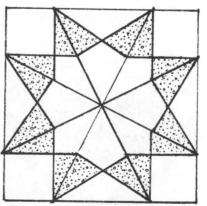

107. St. Louis Star
#4, B-5, D-12, G-4, K-4, K-5

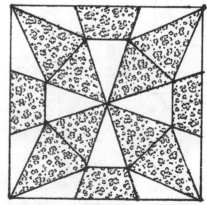

108. Joseph's Coat
#A-12, A-16, D-13, E-7

12-inch Blocks

109. Thrifty Wife
#B-7, G-6, see page 143 for center

110. Bleeding Heart
#3, see page 145

111. Morning Star
#23, 33, A-18, A-19, D-19, D-18, K-2

112. The Crab
#3, 5, A-5, B-8, G-7, K-1

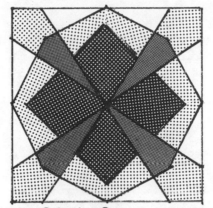

113. Spinning Star
#D-16, D-17, K-8, K-9, K-10

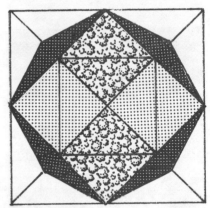

114. Jewel II
#36, D-10, F-9

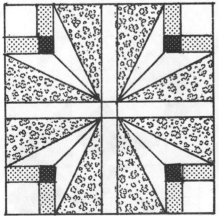

115. Easter Tide (13")
#1, 3, 46, 43, B-7, D-14

116. New Star (13")
#1, 13, 46, A-17, D-15, K-7

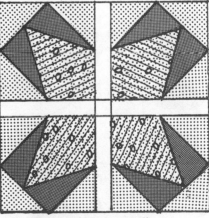

117. Star and Cross (13")
#1, 23, 46, K-6, B-20

12-inch Blocks

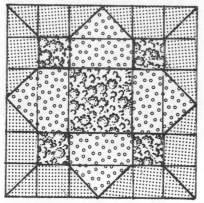

118. Cornerstone
#3, 5, 24, 44

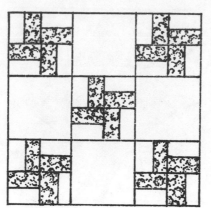

119. Illinois Road
#5, 43

120. Wedding Bouquet
#3, 13, 24, 34

121. Medallion Square
#1, 3, 5, 43

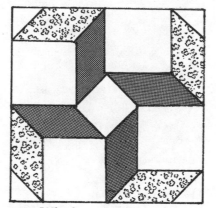

122. Whirlaround
#5, 13, 34, C-5

123. Arrangement of Small Pieces
#24, C-5, E-3

124. Carnival
#5, A-1, A-20, E-10

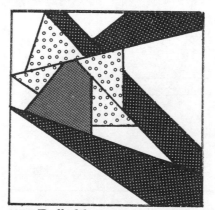

125. Daffodils
See pages 150–153

126. Flying Shuttles
#3, 13, 34

9-inch Blocks

127. Independence Square
#1, 5, 43, 42

128. Window Square
#4, 23, L-19, see page 146

129. Split 9-Patch
#4, 15

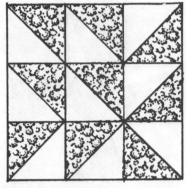

130. Four Clowns
#1, 11, 15, 42

131. Creole Puzzle
#2, 15, 20, 23

132. Windmill
#15

133. Old Snowflake
#4, 13, 23, L-17

134. All Points
#13, 15, 23, 42, L-17

135. Hen and Her Chicks
#1, 4

136. Emma C.
#15, 21, 32, 42, L-23

137. Autograph
#4, 15, B-5, G-5

138. Fair Play
#15, 23, A-11, F-8

139. Wedge and Circle
#4, 11, B-6, N-4, N-5

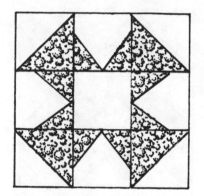

140. A Dandy
#4, 15, B-2, L-24

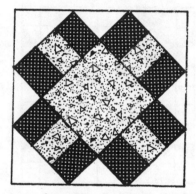

141. Aunt Tryphosa's Favorite
#15, 23, 36, 51

142. Bradford 9-Patch
#1, 4, 42

143. Wedding March I
#1, 11, 13, 42

144. At the Square
#4, 23

9-inch Blocks

145. Dallas Star
#13, 23, 32, A-20, L-25

146. Flag In, Flag Out
#4, M-4

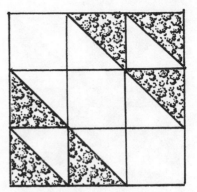

147. Friendship Name Chain
#15, 4

148. 1941 9-Patch
#4, L-19, F-6

149. New 4-Pointer
#4, 15, B-5, F-6, G-6

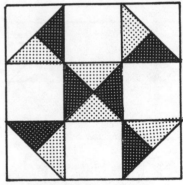

150. Cobwebs
#4, 15, 23

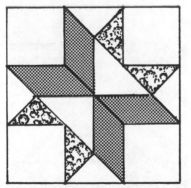

151. Right Hand of Fellowship
#4, 15, 23, C-10

152. Windmill All Around
#1, 11

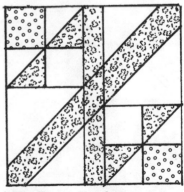

153. Goose Tracks
#3, 13, 15, 17, E-11, 1" x 12"
strip

154. Sunburst I
#1, 11, 42, B-6, D-20

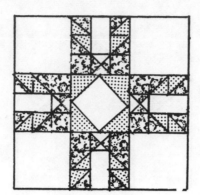

155. Chicago Star
#4, 11, 12, 21, 33, 43

156. Main Street
#1, 42, 11

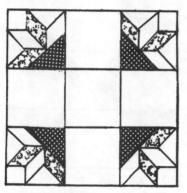

157. Sage Bud
#1, 4, C-11

158. Heather Square
#11, 22, 23, 49, L-5

159. Ribbon Star
#1, 11, 4, 42, 43

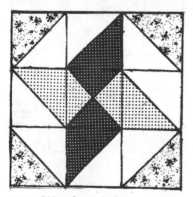

160. Wandering Star
#15, 23

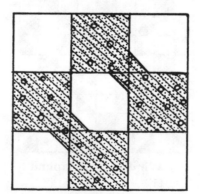

161. Double Necktie
#4, M-5

162. Housewife's Dream
#4, 11, M-6, A-22, A-23

18-inch Blocks

163. Arkansas
#3, 7, 23, 33

164. Texas Treasure
#2, 6, 7, 12, 23, 47

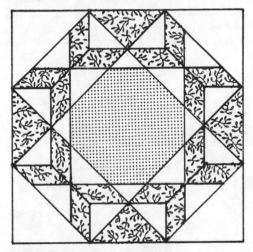

165. Pharlemina's Favorite
#15, 19, 23, 26, C-10, N-8

166. Grandmother's Quilt
#2, 6, 16, 28

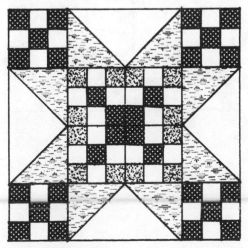

167. Bridle Path
#2, 16, 28

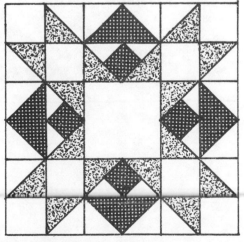

168. Best of All
#4, 7, 15, 23, 26, 33

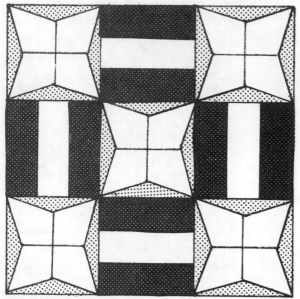

169. Star Spangled Banner
#47, K-4, F-10

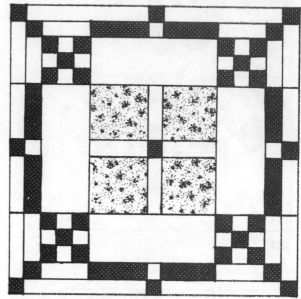

170. Road to California
#1, 5, 41, 42, 1″ × 8″ strip, 3″ × 8″ strip

171. Colonial Garden
#4, 23, 33

172. Bear's Den
#3, 13, 19, 45

173. Pine Tree
#4, A-18, B-5

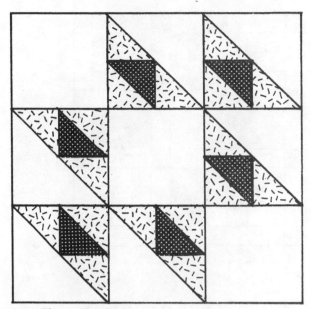

174. Flying Bird
#7, 15, 19

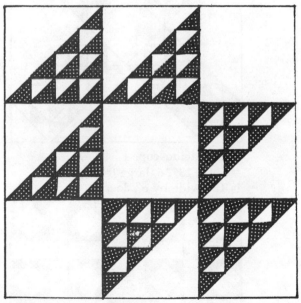

175. Double Pyramid
#7, 12, 15

176. Mona's Choice
#7, A-18, A-21, K-4

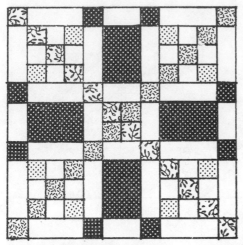

177. King's Highway
#2, 42, 53

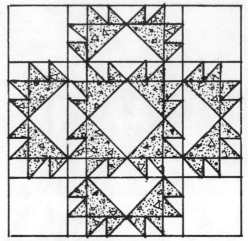

178. Wedding March
#2, 12, 15, 23, 26, 36

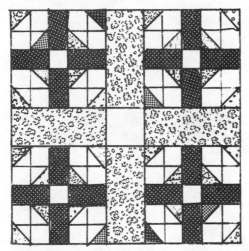

179. A Scrap Patch
#2, 4, 12, 54, 55

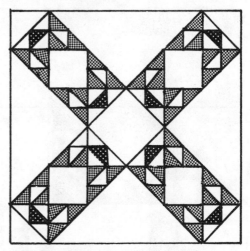

180. Kaleidoscope I
#4, 12, 15, 36, large triangle
is 12″ wide by 6″ deep

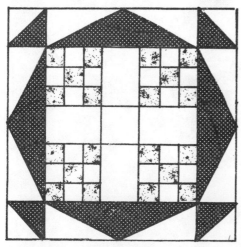

181. Quilt Without a Name
#2, 4, 15, 53, B-7

182. Economy
#2, 12, 32, 54, 55

8-inch Blocks

183. Give This One a Name
#3, 17

184. Sickle
#3, 17

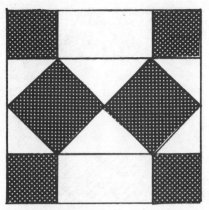

185. Belle's Favorite
#3, 13, 24, 34, 44

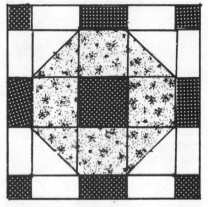

186. Going Home
#1, 3, 13, 43

187. Aimée's Choice
#15, 22, A-15, E-13, K-11

188. Wheel of Fortune
#3, K-12, L-29, M-5, N-6

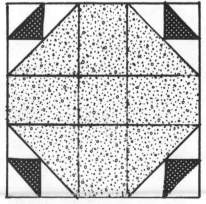

189. Happy New Year II
#3, 12, 15, 49

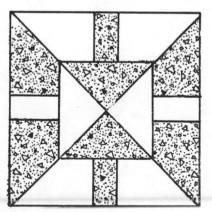

190. Twin Darts
#24, 43, L-32

191. Pale Star
#3, 13, 24

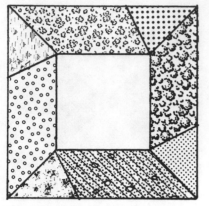

192. Road to Berlin
#5, 24, C-5

193. Star of the West
#13, 24, 34

194. Winged Square
#13, 24, 34

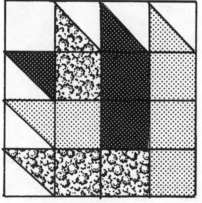

195. Pineapple Plant
#3, 13

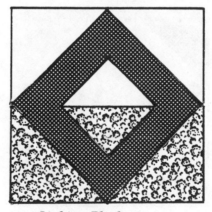

196. Linking Blocks
#17, 24, E-2

197. Flywheel
#13, 17, 34

12-inch Blocks

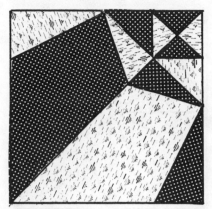

198. Allentown (8″)
#13, 22, B-1, B-9, N-7

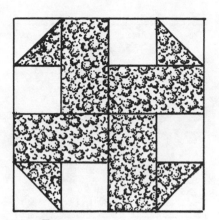

199. Zigzag
#4, 15, 47

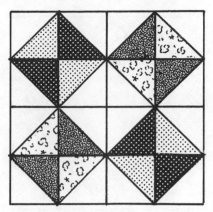

200. Fox and Goose
#15

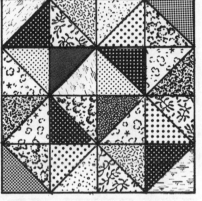

201. Flying Colors
#15

202. Road to Damascus
#4, 15, 23, 26, 33

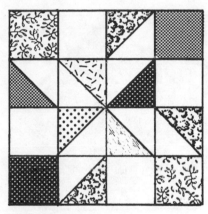

203. Meteor
#4, 15

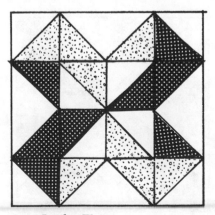

204. Lucky Pieces
#15, 26

205. Aunt Nancy's Favorite
#15, 23, 26, 36, 56

206. Summer's Dream
#3, 4, 12, 26

12-inch Blocks

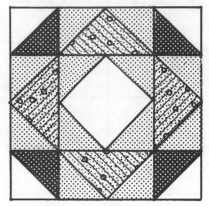

207. Canadian Gardens
#15, 26, 36

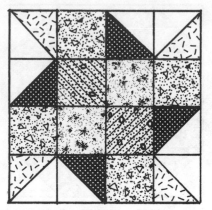

208. Churn Dash
#4, 15

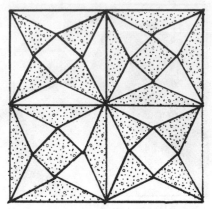

209. Golden Wedding
#33, A-24, F-10

210. Anvil
#4, 15, L-30, E-14

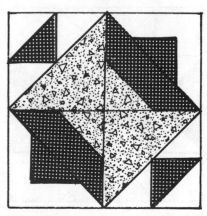

211. Kite
#15, 19, E-14

212. Hourglass
#15, 36

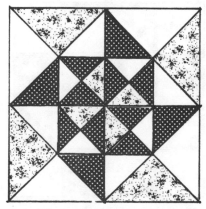

213. Marion's Choice
#15, 23, 26

214. Martha's Choice
#15, 23, 26

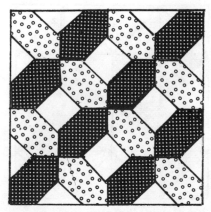

215. Road to Tennessee
#23, 33, L-31

12-inch Blocks

216. Whirling Squares
#23, 33

217. Boston Belle
#3, 25, 57, A-27, E-17

218. Chain and Bar
#12, 16, 23, 53

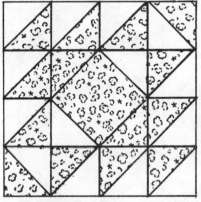

219. Doublecross II
#15, 36

220. Empire Star
#15, 19, 36

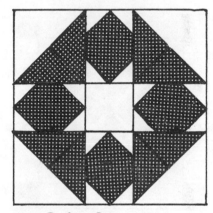

221. Goshen Star
#4, 12, 16, L-33

222. Miller's Daughter
#2, 4, 12, 55, N-8

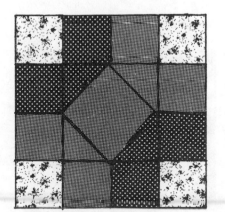

223. Y-Bridge
#4, 15, 36

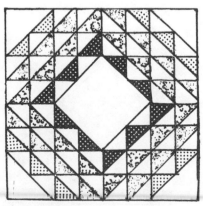

224. Jubilee
#2, 15, 36

12-inch Blocks

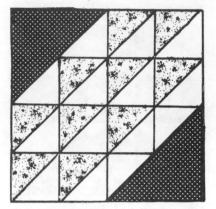

225. Migration
#15, 19

226. True Lover's Knot
#4, A-25, A-26, E-15, E-16,
L-34, L-35, L-36

227. Modern Tulip
#2, 12, 58, 59, 60, C-7, D-8,
K-13, L-37

228. Midsummer Garden
#2, 23, D-21, K-6A, K-9A, L-19

229. Twist Patchwork
#12, 23, 33, N-8

230. Mosaic II
#15, 26, 36

231. H-Square
#15, 19, see page 144, 36

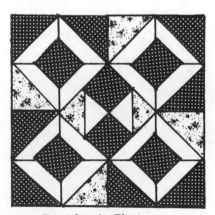

232. President's Choice
#15, 33, E-18

233. Chain of Diamonds
#2, B-5, F-10, K-4, N-9

12-inch Blocks

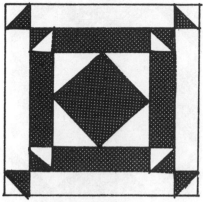

234. Double Squares
#12, 15, 36, 46, 1½" x 9" strip

235. Apple Tree
#2, 12, 15, C-10, see page 144

236. Star
#2, 4, 12, 23, C-7

237. Pigs in a Blanket
#15

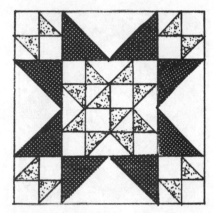

238. Coronation
#2, 12, 15, 23, 26

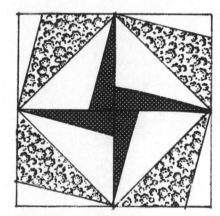

239. Perpetual Motion
#B-11, D-22

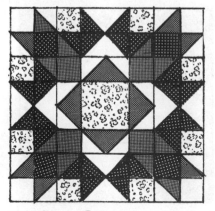

240. Arrow Crown
#2, 4, 12, 23

241. Beacon Lights
#23, 25, A-18, B-10, 11, L-39, 22

242. Ohio Star
#4, 15, 33, C-10

12-inch Blocks

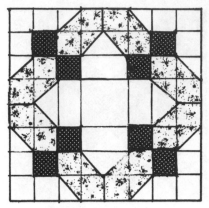

243. Thirteen Squares
#2, 4, 11, 23

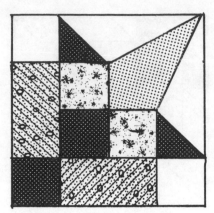

244. Rocket Ship
#4, 15, 47, K-14, B-7

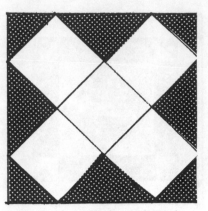

245. Quilt in Light and Dark
#15, 26, 36

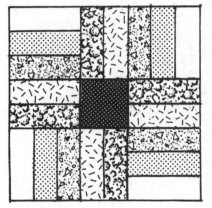

246. Paddle Wheel
#58, 4

247. Far Horizons
#12, 15, 23, 33, C-10

248. Acorns
#12, 23, 55

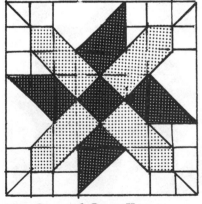

249. Star and Cross II
#2, 12, 15, 23, 33, D-23

250. Sunlight and Shadows
#4, 15, 23

251. Star of Four Points
#5, A-1, A-28, K-6B

12-inch Blocks

252. Symmetry in Motion
#15, 26, 36

253. Tulip Time
#D-10A, F-11, F-12,
see pages 148-150

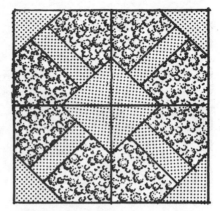

254. Spider Web
#15, 36, 57, L-41

255. Lily of the Field
#4, A-18, K-4, M-5

256. Chalice
#A-18, B-7, C-14, F-10, F-11,
F-12

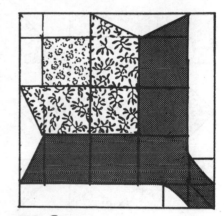

257. Crocus
#2, 4, 12, 43, B-5, F-19,
1½″ × 9″ strip

258. To Market, to Market
#4, 15, 36

259. Wheel of Time
#15, 26

260. Snowflake
#4, 15

12-inch Blocks

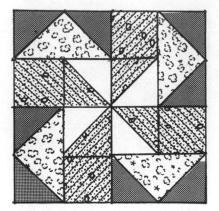

261. Seesaw
#15, 26

262. Boise
#15, 26, 36, 47

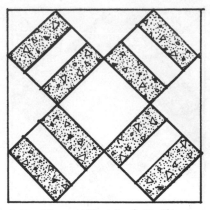

263. House That Jack Built
#15, 26, 36, 61

264. Star and Arrows
#13, 15, 26, L-38

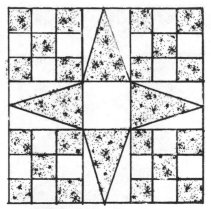

265. Stepping-Stones
#2, 4, B-12

266. Bismarck
#4, 12, L-43

267. Arrowhead
#26, 33, see L-26

268. Butterfly
#15, 26, 36

269. Basket of Lilies
#2, 4, 12, 15, B-20, 26, C-11

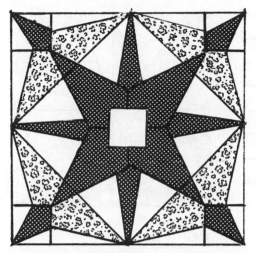

270. West Virginia
#3, A-29, B, D-24, D-25, K-2, K-16

271. Western Spy
#17, 20C, C-15, D-26, F-13, F-14

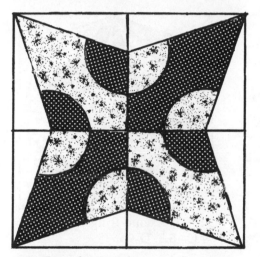

272. Caps for Witches and Dunces
#B-13, see page 155

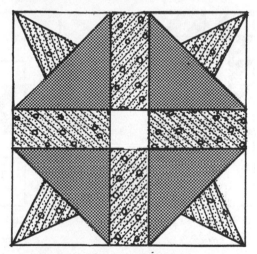

273. Block of Many Triangles
#3, 18, 45A, A-30, D-9

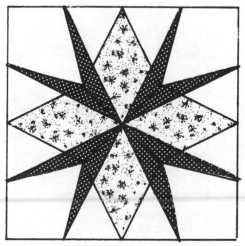

274. Stars over Texas
#A-18, C-14, F-15, K-6

275. Lady of the White House
#2, 4, 15

12-inch Blocks

276. Kites in the Air (continuous strips) #12, 23, A-18, B-5

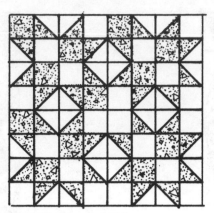

277. Cubes and Tiles #2, 12

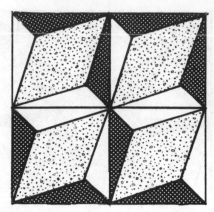

278. Blue Boutonnieres #C-16, D-9

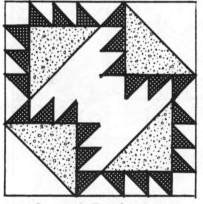

279. Lawyer's Puzzle #2, 12, 16

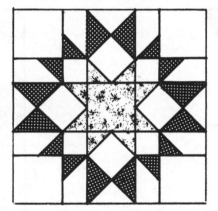

280. Green Mountain Star #2, 4, 12, 23, 33

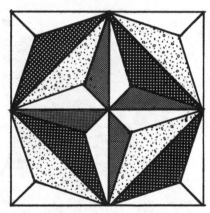

281. Diamond Ring I #C-16A, D-9

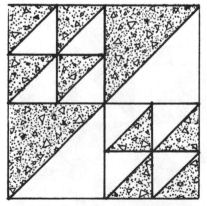

282. Flock of Geese #15, 19

283. Salt Lake City I #15, 23, 33, 36

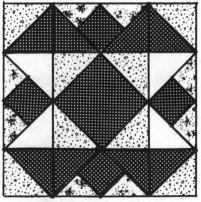

284. Mosaic III #15, 23, 26, 33, 36

12-inch Blocks

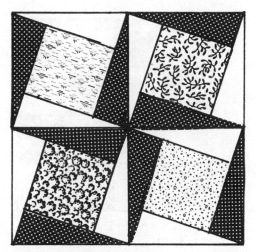

285. Radio Windmill
See page 159

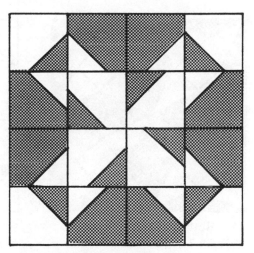

286. Columbian Puzzle
#13, M-6

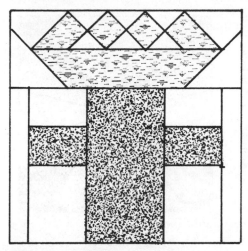

287. Cross and Crown I
#15, 22, 32, 49, D-27, E-20, 1″ × 8″
strips

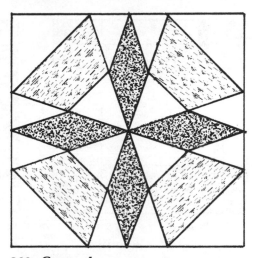

288. Concord
#17, A-9, A-31, C-18, E-21

289. Lover's Lane
#3, 13, 34

290. Our Next President
#15, 33, E-18

12-inch Blocks

291. Rolling Star
#33, A-24, F-10

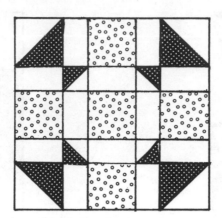

292. Table for Four
#4, 12, 15, 55

293. Housewife II
#2, 4, 12, 15

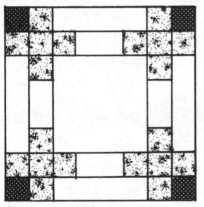

294. Rosebud
#2, 7, 55, 1½″ × 6″ strip

295. Old Spanish Tile
#2, 12, 23, A-23, 1½″ × 6″ strip

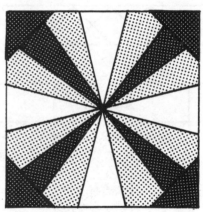

296. Nova
#15, A-32, A-33, A-34

297. Sparkling Crystals
#31, A-24, C-14, D-28, F-12

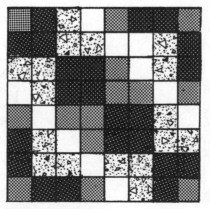

298. Steps to Glory
#12

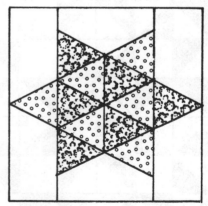

299. Six-Point Star
#A-18, N-9, L-50

12-inch Blocks

300. Cheyenne
#4, 15, 36

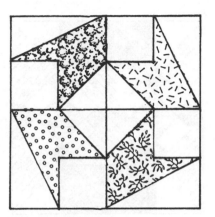

301. Fancy Foot
#4, 36, B-7, 15

302. Cypress
#7, 15, see page 159

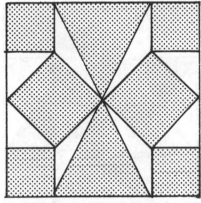

303. Butterfly in Angles
#4, 15, 36, A-35, D-14

304. Milkmaid's Star
#15, 36, A-11, E-22

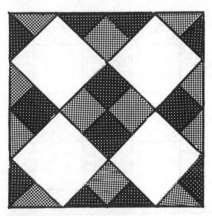

305. Salute to the Colors
#23, 33, 36

306. Signature
#29A, L-43

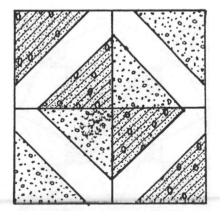

307. Golden Memories
#16, L-40A

308. Lucky Star
#A-24, C-14, C-18, F-10

12-inch Blocks

309. Lena's Choice
#4, 22, 23, C-17

310. Peace and Plenty
#15, 26, 31, 33, 47, 62

311. World's Prize
#15, 23, 33

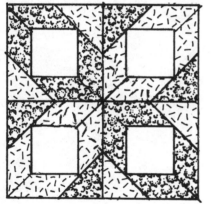

312. This 'n That I
#4, 15, C-10

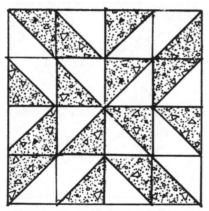

313. Squire Smith's Choice
#15

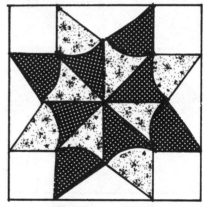

314. Sailor's Joy
#15, F-10, see page 156

315. Salt Lake City II
#7, 15, 23, 33, 57

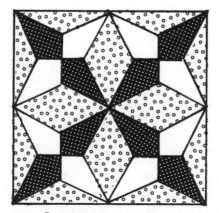

316. Sacramento
#C-14, F-10, K-4

317. Kentucky Chain
#23, L-38, L-40A

12-inch Blocks

318. Scotch Plaid
#15, 23, 36, 57

319. Star of the Milky Way
#15

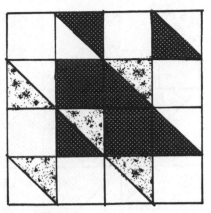

320. Wild Duck
#4, 15

321. Forgotten Star
#23, 36, A-36, D-29

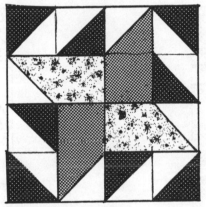

322. Pinwheel II
#4, 15

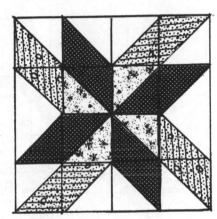

323. Poinsettia
#4, 15

324. Rosepoint
#A-3, D-10, K-17, see page 156

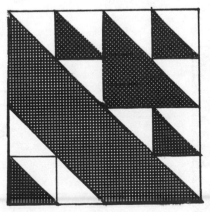

325. Airplane I
#15, 19

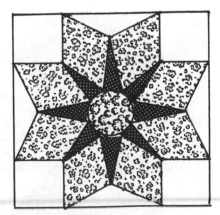

326. Sunflower
#4, F-10, see page 157

12-inch Blocks

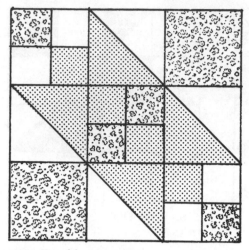

327. Double Hourglass
#3, 5, 17

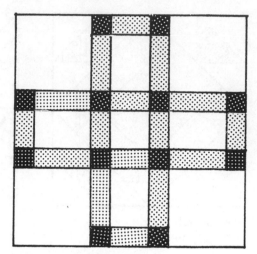

328. Tic-Tac-Toe
#1, 2, 5, 43, 42, 49

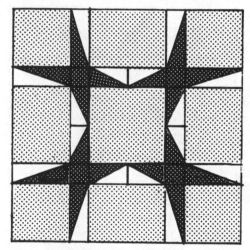

329. Acrobats
#1, 5, B, B-6

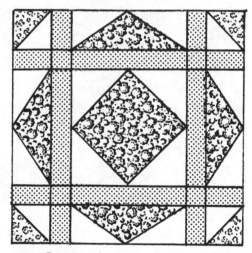

330. Crossroads
#1, 13, 15, 36, 43, 46, B-8, F-16

331. Kentucky Patch
#1, 13, 24

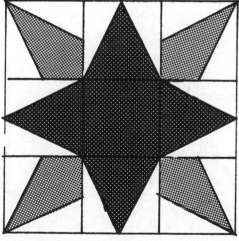

332. Starburst
#5, A-1, B-1, K-1

12-inch Blocks

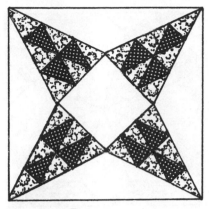

333. Pine Burr
#36, A-37, F-12A

334. Albany
#15, 23, 33, C-10

335. Bowbells
#15, 21, 23, 31, 33, 43

336. Blazing Arrows
#15

337. Flower Bed
#23, 33, 29B

338. Puerto Rico
#2, 15, 36

339. Plain Sailing
#16, A-38, B-16, L-19

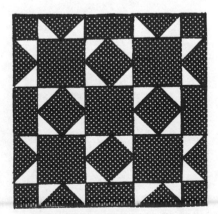

340. Glitter, Glitter
#2, 4, 12, 23, 33, 55A

341. Trails
#4, 15, 26

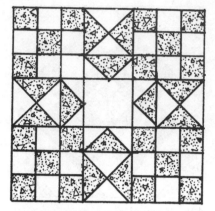

342. Winged 9-Patch
#3, 5, 24

343. Reverse X
#24

344. In the Arbor
#24, C-5, K-18, K-19

345. Spider Legs
#24, A-1, C-5, D-22A

346. Three Cheers
#5, 13, 17, 24, 66, E-2, L-44

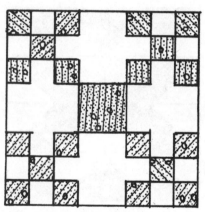

347. Nine-Patch Variation
#3, 5, 2″ × 6″ piece

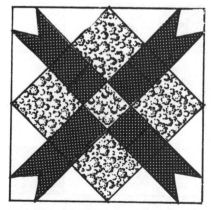

348. Royal Star
#26, 34, 39, K-6B, L-45

349. San Diego
#3, 5, 13, 17, 24

350. Bear's Paw
#3, 13, 19

16-inch Blocks

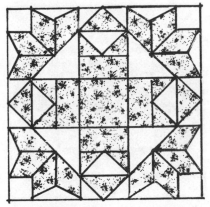

351. Sunburst II
#3, 5, 13, 17, 24, 44, D-30

352. Five Square
#3, 5, 13, 24, 44, 63

353. New Barrister Block
#3, 5, 13

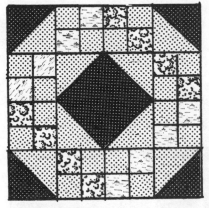

354. Irish Chain
#3, 17, 39

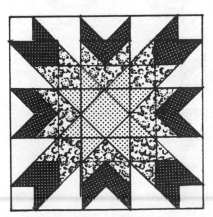

355. Christmas Star II
#3, 13, 17, 24, 34

356. World's Fair
#13, 34, F-6, G, L-49

357. Double Tulip
#3, 24, 34, 44, C-18, see page 153

358. Baskets (diagonal set)
#3, 13, 19, 45

359. Cabbage Rose
#13, 24, 34, B-1, F-16, F-17, F-18

360. Images
#3, 13, 17, 28, 34

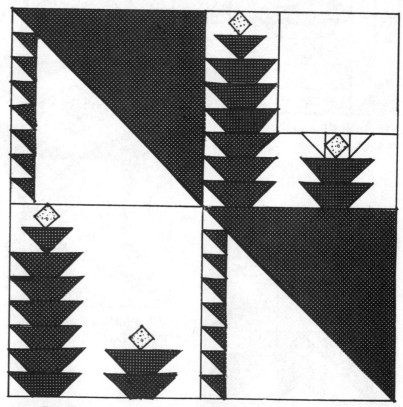

361. Farmer's Fields
#17, 24, 34, C-18

362. Candles
#13, 24, 32, 14″ triangle, 16″ triangle, 10″ square, E-9

16-inch Blocks

363. Tulip
#3, 13, 17, 24, 34, 44

364. Album Flower
#3, 24, 34, A-1, B, D-8, K-20, L-46

365. Dinah's Choice
#15, 19, 24, 26, 34, A-31, B-9

366. Diamond Ring II
#3, 5, 13, 17, 24, 44

367. Home Treasure
#5, 13, 17, 24, 39, 44

368. Kaleidoscope II
#3, 13, 24, 44

369. Around the Corner
#5, 17, 24, 34

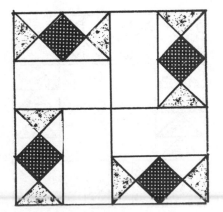

370. Flying Fish
#24, 34, 4″ × 8″ rectangle

371. Lightning
#3, 7, 13, 4″ × 8″ rectangle

16-inch Blocks

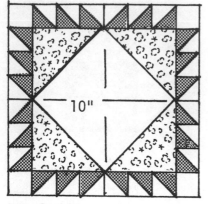

372. Sunshine
#2, 13, 19, see instructions for center

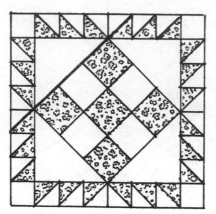

373. Spring Has Come
#3, 13, 19, 34

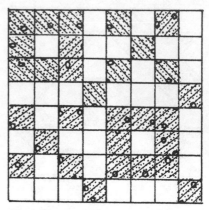

374. Crossword Puzzle
#3

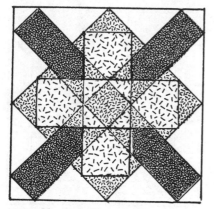

375. Shaded Crossroad
#2, 22, 24, 26, 34, 44, L-12

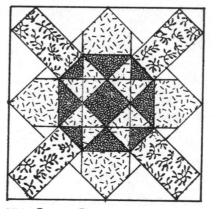

376. Starry Cross
#2, 22, 24, 26, 44, 34, L-12A

377. Lily
#3, 13, 19, 24, 34, 44

378. Friendship Star
#3, 5, 13, 24, 44

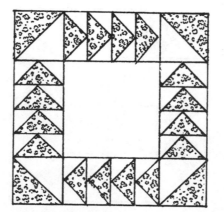

379. Fox and Geese
8" square, #13, 17, 24

380. Footbridge
#3, 13, 24, 44, 4" × 8" rectangle

16-inch Blocks

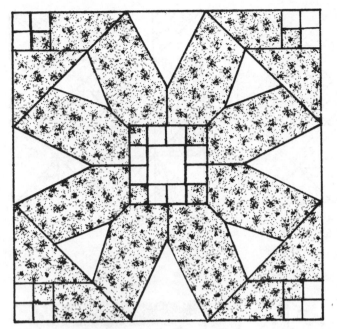

381. Sue's Delight
#1, 5, 17, A, A-1, L-14, L-44, L-47

382. Aunt Lucinda's Double Irish Chain
#7, 13, 32, 34

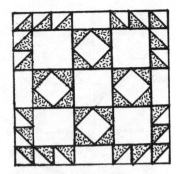

383. Mineral Wells
#5, 13, 34, 44

384. Monterey
#5, 24, A-1, B-1, C-5

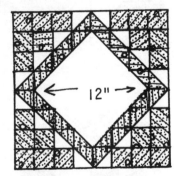

385. Memory Block
#3, 13

386. Duck Tracks
#3, 5, 13, 24, 34, 44

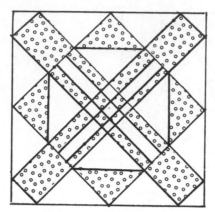

387. Sonnie's Playhouse
#1, 13, 26, 64, 66A

388. Design for Patriotism
#17, 24, 32

389. Double Square
#17, 24, A-39, C-5, K-21

390. Dove in the Window
#17, A-1, A-40, C-19, D-31, F-17

391. Square Diamond
#13, 24, 34, E-9, E-23

392. Broken Crystals
#5, 24, A-1, B-1, B-15, D-31, K-1

393. Triangles and Squares
#3, 13, 17, 22, 24, 32

394. This 'n That II
#5, 17, 24

10-inch Blocks

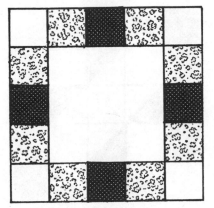

395. Multiple Squares
#3, 7

396. May Basket
#3, 13, 24, 17, 45

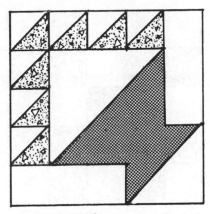

397. Fruit Basket
#13, 19, 45, 17

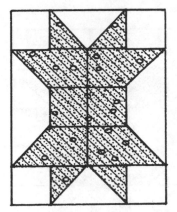

398. Sylvia's Bow (8 × 10)
#3, 13, 24

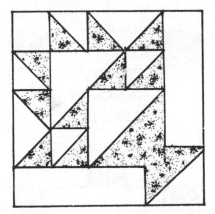

399. Flower Basket
#3, 13, 24, 17, 65, D-33, 15

400. Heavenly Problem
#3, 13, 44, A-6, D-34, K-7A

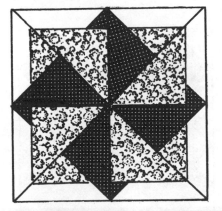

401. Tumbleweed
#17, 22, 24, E-24

402. Prized Possession
#3, 13, B, C

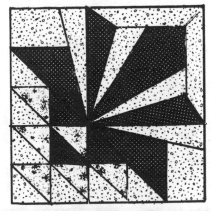

403. Leafy Basket
#13, E-3A, see page 158

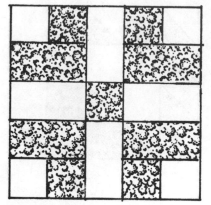

404. Double V
#3

405. Fair and Square
#1, 3, 13, 34, 41, 43, 44

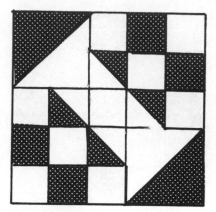

406. Spool
#3, 13, 17

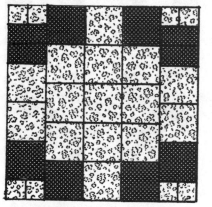

407. Jericho Walls
#3, 7, 43

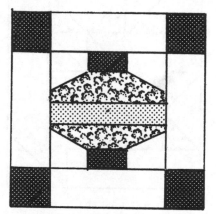

408. Japanese Gardens
#3, 45, 46, 43, see page 144

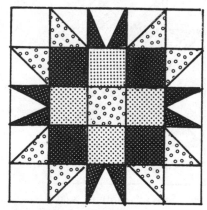

409. Triangle Puzzle
#3, 13, A-5, B

410. Friendship
#22, 32, L-48

411. Album
#22, 13, 32

412. Domino and Square
#13, 22, 32

10-inch Blocks

413. Airplane II
#3, 11, 22, 41, 45, A-1, B-1, E-1, L-32A

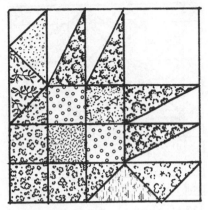

414. Fish
#3, 13, 24, B-1

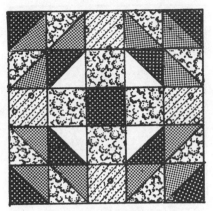

415. Odd Scraps Patchwork
#3, 13

416. Altar Candle
#3, 13, 17, 19, 45

417. Sewing Circle
#13, A-41, B-17, 46A

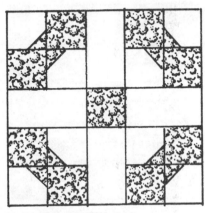

418. Carrie's Choice
#3, 11, 44, M-5

419. Brock House
#3, 5

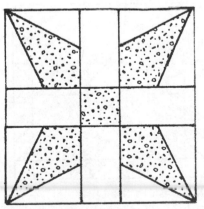

420. King David's Crown
#3, 44, B-1, K-1

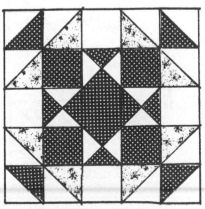

421. Maine Woods
#3, 13, 22, 34

10-inch Blocks

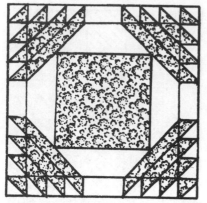

422. Pine Burr II
#8, 11, 15, 43, E-25

423. Cathedral Window
#1, 3, 11, 13, 22, 34, 43

424. Grandmother Percy's Puzzle
#3, 13, 17, 44

425. Granny's Favorite
#1, 3, 11, 24, 43

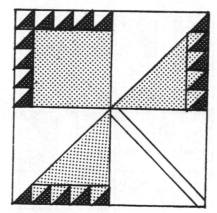

426. Broken Branch
#5, 8, 11, bias for stem

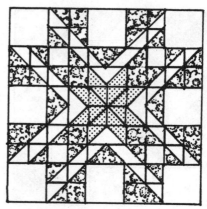

427. Leavenworth Star
#1, 3, 11, 22

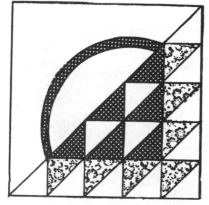

428. Basket
#13, 10" triangle, see page 142

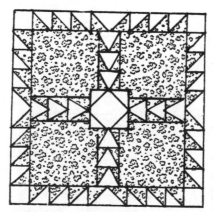

429. Fish in the Dish
#1, 11, 22, 32, A-39, B-17

430. Posy Plot
#1, 11, 22, 32, 42, 43

10-inch Blocks

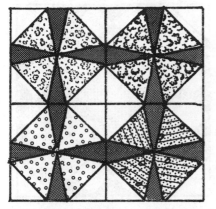

431. King's Cross
#13, A-41A, A-42

432. Old Maid's Puzzle I
#11, 17, 43, see page 142

433. Four Diamonds (continuous design) #B-18, C-20

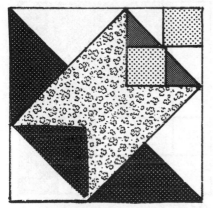

434. Trumpet Flower
#3, 12, 26, E-26

435. Beacon
#11, 15, 21, 49, D-35

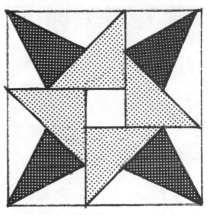

436. Spinning Star
#3, 17, A-3, B-1, D-36

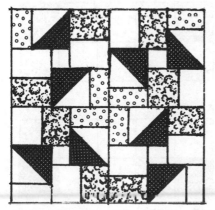

437. Hedgerow
#1, 13, 43, 55A

438. Nine-Patch Design
#3, 11, 22, 32, 45

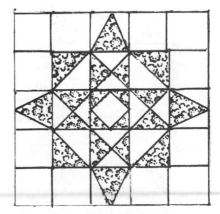

439. King of the Mountain
#3, 13, 22, 32, A-5, B

440. Polly's Favorite
#3, 13, 22, 32, 34

441. Lewis and Clark
#3, 13, 22, 32, 34

442. Domino and Star
#13, 22, 32, 34

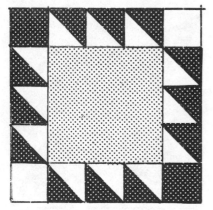

443. Double Sawtooth
#3, 7, 13

444. Marion's Choice
#3, 13

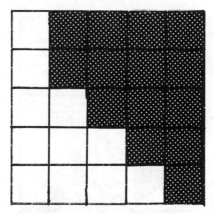

445. Sunshine and Shadow
#3

446. Souvenir
#3, 7, 13

447. Hills of Vermont
#13, 19

448. Bright Jewel
#3, 13

10-inch Blocks

449. Mona and Monette
#1, 44

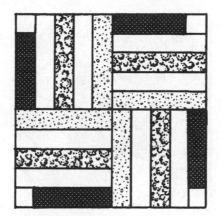

450. California
#1, 41, 46A

451. Ozark Trail
#1, 13

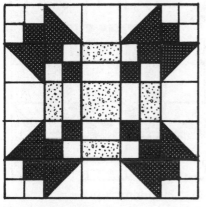

452. Gamecocks
#1, 3, 13, 43

453. Woodland Path
#11, 17, 22, 32

454. Sunbeam Crossroad
#11, 22, 24, 32

455. Squares
#3, 11, 22, 32, 46

456. Starry Lane
#1, 3, 13, 24, 43

457. Pinwheel II
#13, 15

458. Broken Heart
#3, 11, 15, 22, 43, D-27, L-53

459. Wisconsin
#3, 13, 22, A-9, A-31

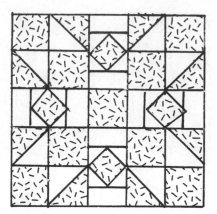

460. Rocky Mountain Chain
#3, 11, 13, 43

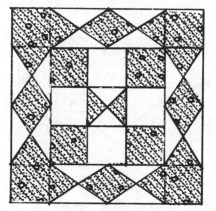

461. Uncle Sam's Hourglass
#3, 22, C-18, C-18A, F-19

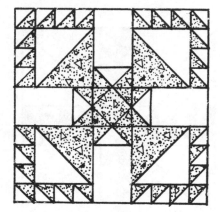

462. Uncle Sam's Favorite
#3, 11, 15, 22, 49

463. Harmony Square
#1, 3, 11, 13, 17, 43

464. Square Dance
#3, 13, N-8

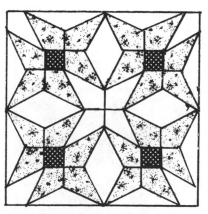

465. Castor and Pollux
#K-2, C, divide C lengthwise
for edge

466. Rustic Wheel
#5, C-22, D-37, E-27, E-28

14-inch Blocks

467. Doves in the Window
#3, 5, 13

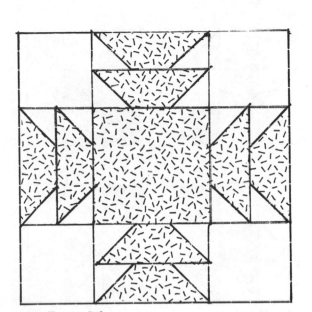

468. Easter Lily
#5, 7, 13, E-9

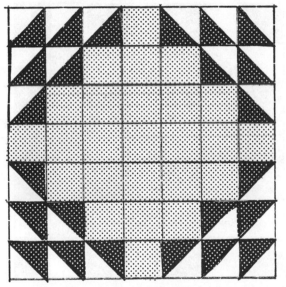

469. Old Maid's Puzzle II
#3, 13

470. Cross and Crown II
#3, 13, 17, 24

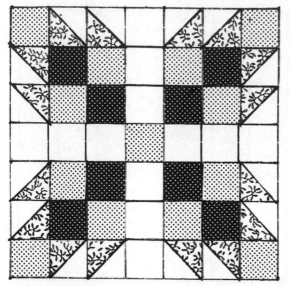

471. Rosebuds
#3, 13

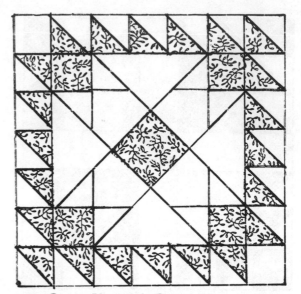

472. Queen Victoria's Crown
#3, 13, 26, 34, L-54

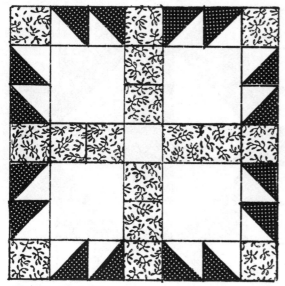

473. Path of Thorns
#3, 5, 13

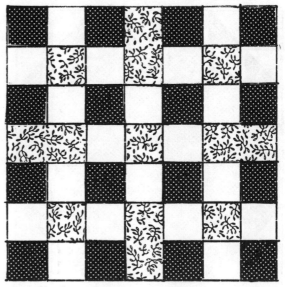

474. Shadow Cross
#3

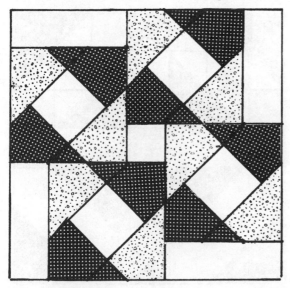

475. Four Square
#3, 22, 34, 45, L-54, D-23A

476. Chain Link
#3, 5

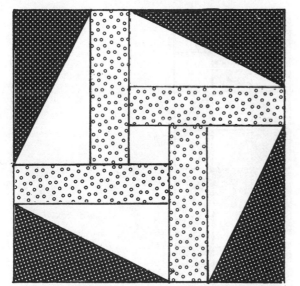

477. Lacy Latticework
#3, B-19

478. Diamond Cross
#3, 13, 44, A-5, B

479. Our Country
#3, 13, A-5, B

480. My Country for Loyalty
#3, 13, 17, 22, 44

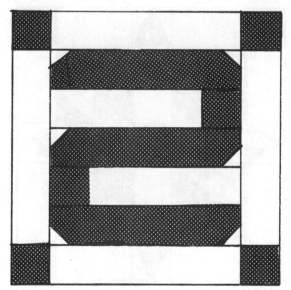

481. Mountain Road
#3, 11, 2″ × 8″ strip, 2″ × 10″ strip

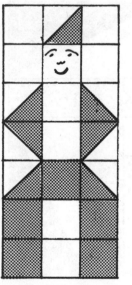

482. Soldier Boy (6″ × 14″ block)
#3, 13

BORDERS

483. Braided Border
4" wide #5, 17
6" wide #7, 19

484. Cupid's Arrowpoint
4" wide #17, 24, 34
6" #19, 26, 36

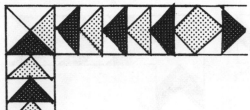

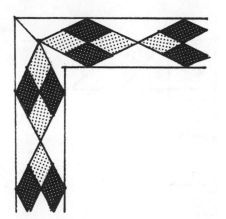

485. Flying Geese
4" #17, 24, 34
6" #19, 26, 36

486. 9-Patch Strip
6" #3, 2" strip
9" #5, 3" strip

487. Four Diamonds
4" #C, D36, G

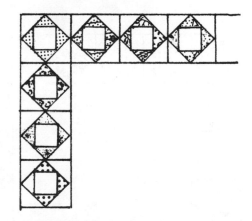

488. Variable Star Border
4" #3, 13, 22
6" #4, 15, 23

489. Triangles
6" #3, A-39, B-1, D-37, D-38

490. Tree Everlasting
6" #7, 15, 2" wide ½ strip

491. Border Design
6" #15, 23, 26, 56

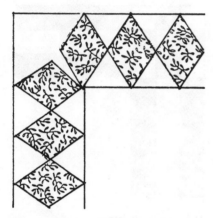

492. Border
6" #C-9, A-43, A-44

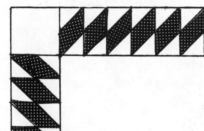

493. Border
4" #5, 13
6" #7, 15

494. Chevron
4" #5, 13
6" #7, 15

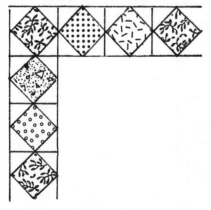

495. Border
4" #13, 34

496. Zigzag
6" #15, 19

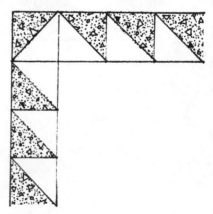

497. Sawtooth
3" #15

498. Pinwheel
6" #15

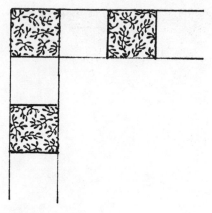

499. Border
3" #4

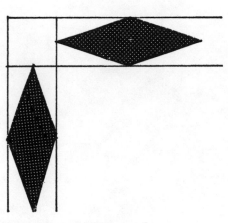

500. Star and Diamond
#3, C-18, B-6

PATTERN PIECES

Add seam allowances to all pattern pieces.

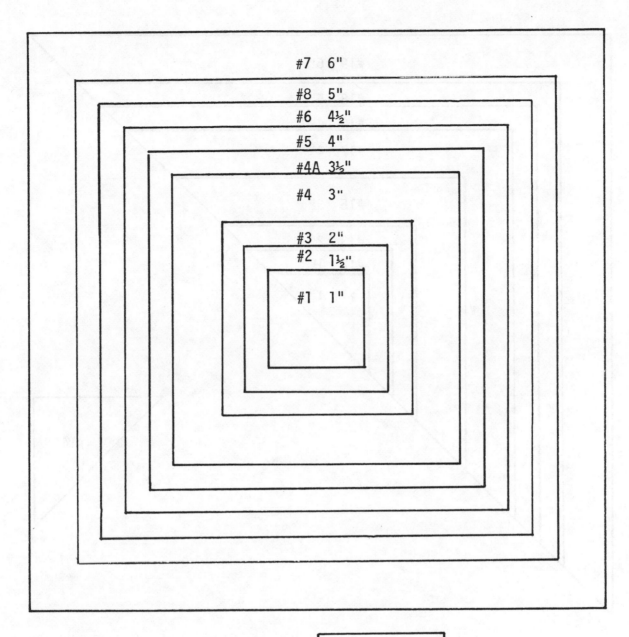

#7   6"

#8   5"

#6   4½"

#5   4"

#4A   3½"

#4   3"

#3   2"

#2   1½"

#1   1"

#9

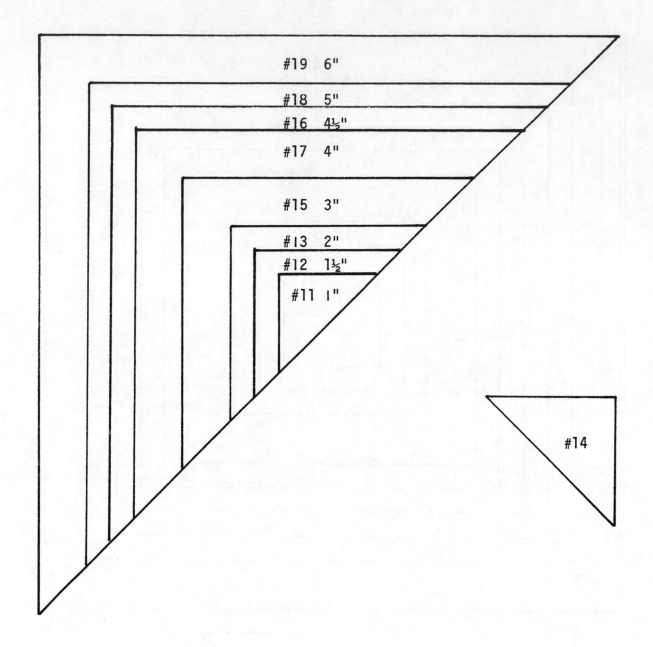

#19 6"

#18 5"

#16 4½"

#17 4"

#15 3"

#13 2"

#12 1½"

#11 1"

#14

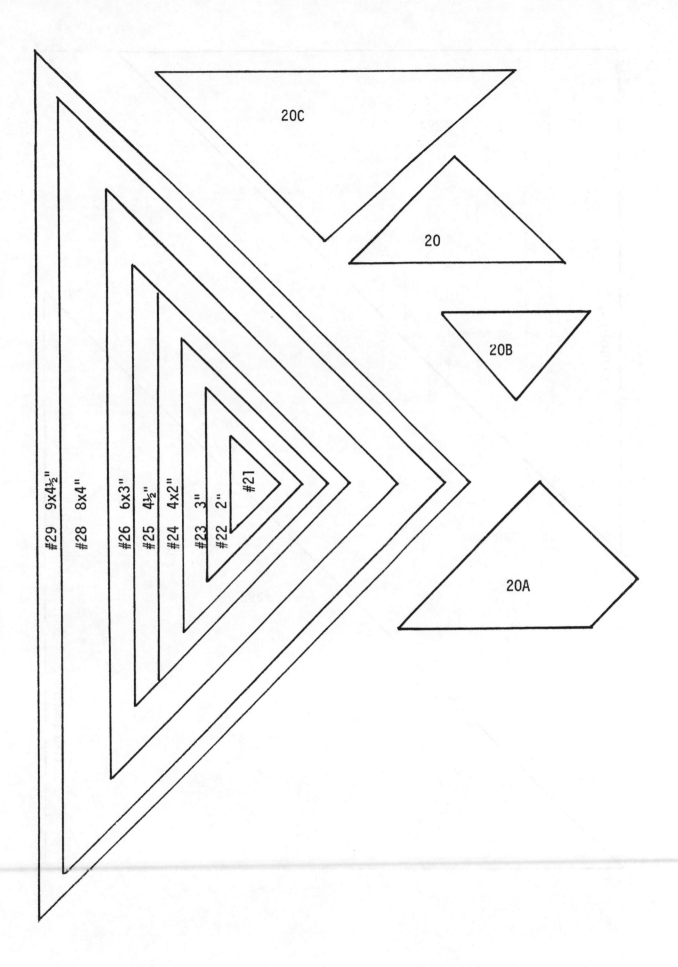

20C

20

20B

20A

#29 9x4½"

#28 8x4"

#26 6x3"

#25 4½"

#24 4x2"

#23 3"

#22 2"

#21

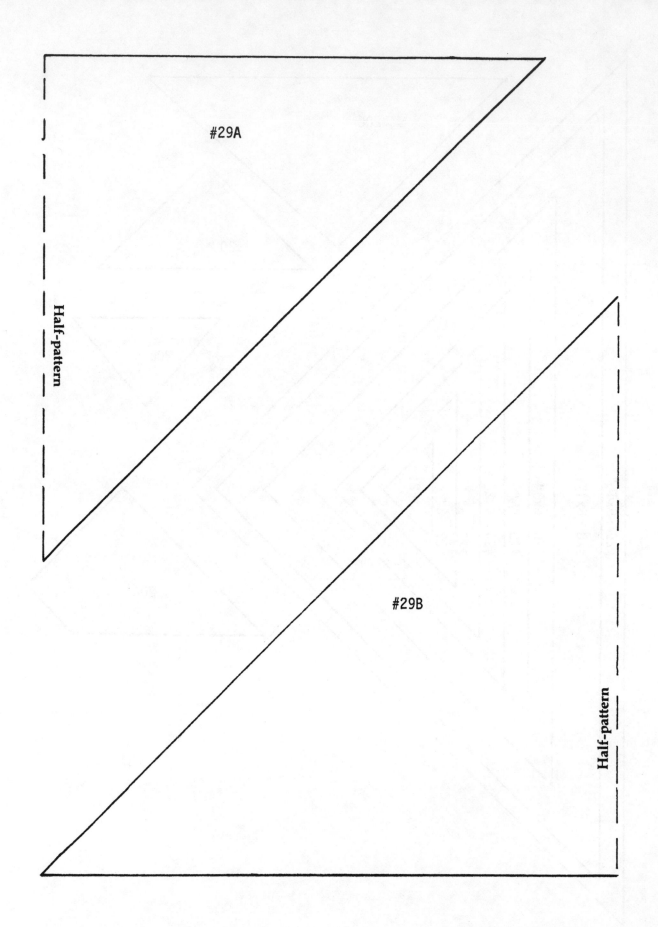

#29A

Half-pattern

#29B

Half-pattern

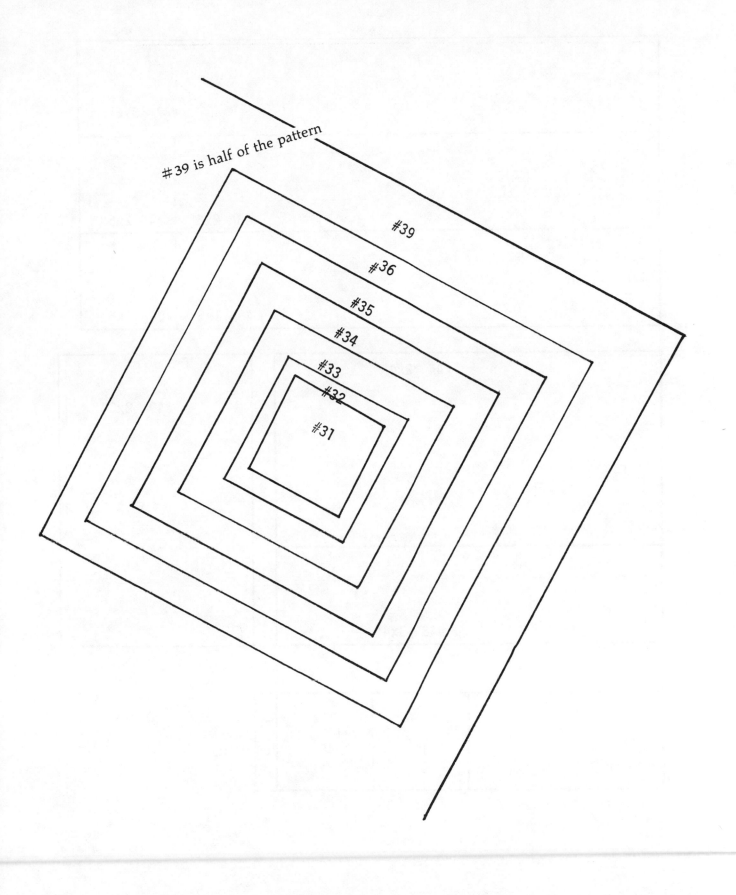

#39 is half of the pattern

#39

#36

#35

#34

#33

#32

#31

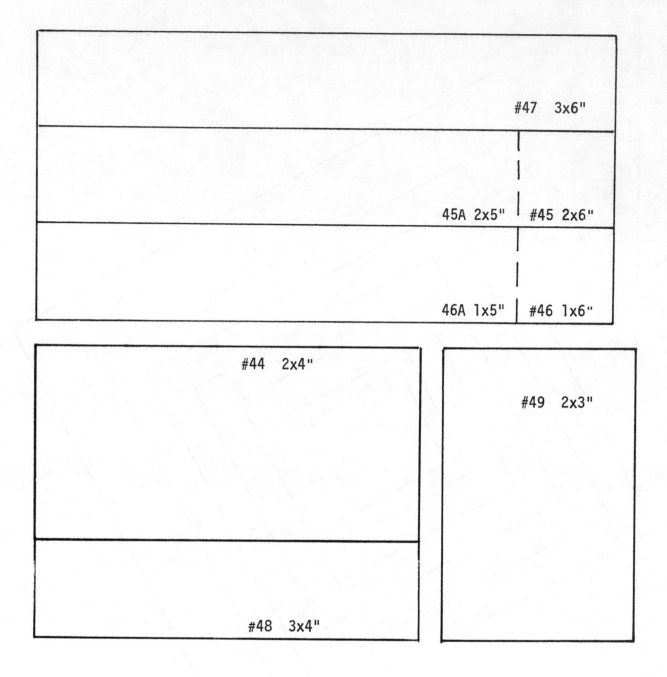

#47   3x6"

45A 2x5"   #45 2x6"

46A 1x5"   #46 1x6"

#44   2x4"

#49   2x3"

#48   3x4"

#43   1x2"   #42   #41   #64 1x4¼"
                1x3"   1x4"

#52   4½x1"

#58   4½ x 1½"

#60   4½ x 2¼"

#53   4½ x 3"

#59   4½ x 7½"

#50

#51

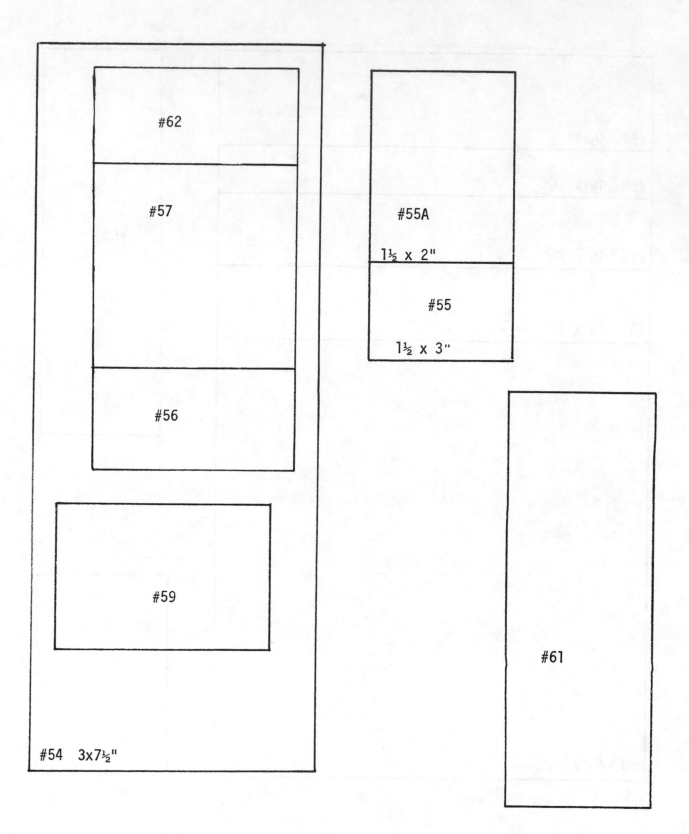

#62

#57

#56

#59

#54   3x7½"

#55A

1½ x 2"

#55

1½ x 3"

#61

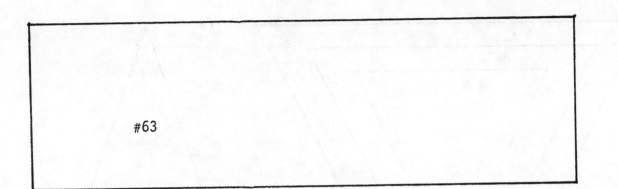

#63

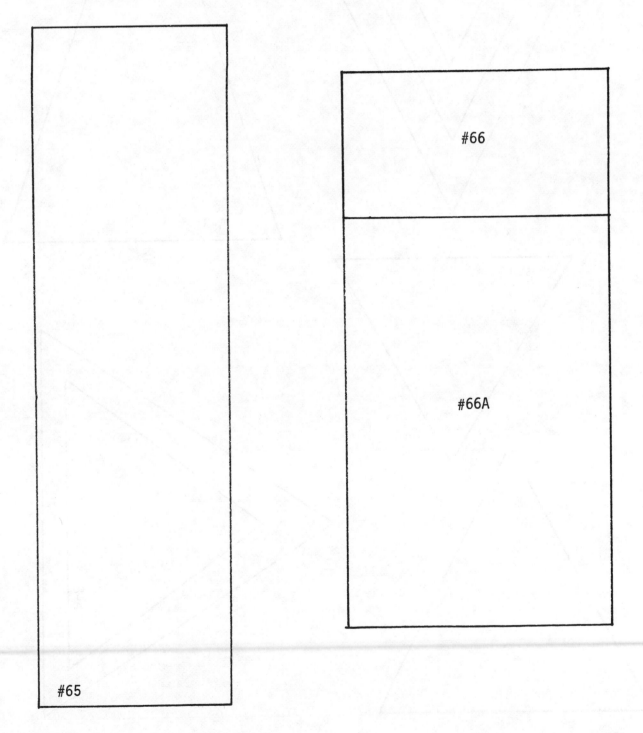

#65

#66

#66A

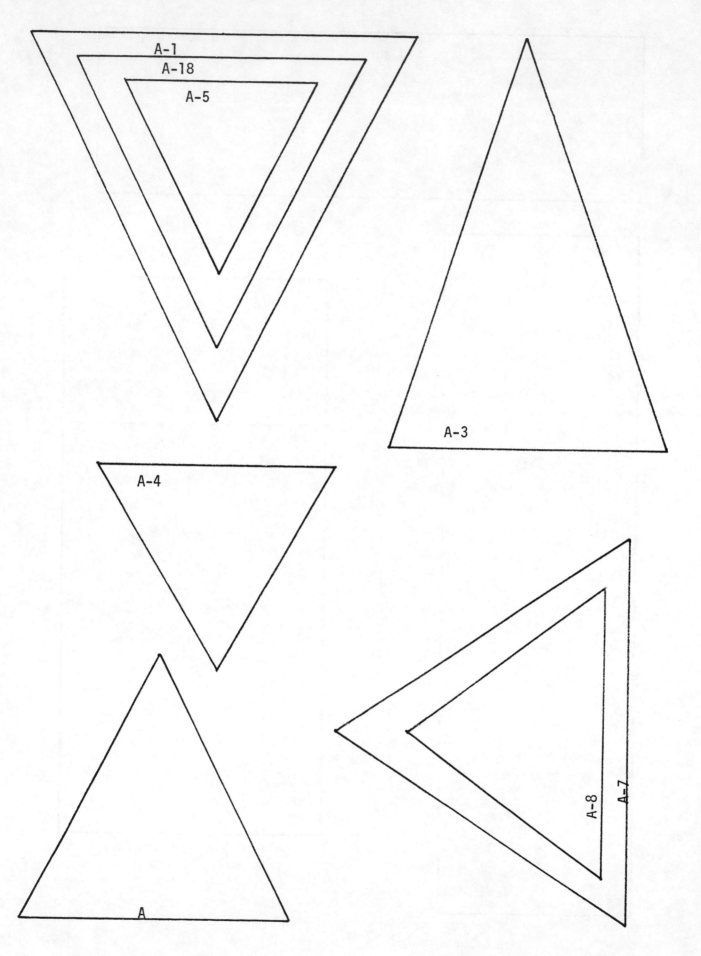

A-1

A-18

A-5

A-3

A-4

A-8

A-7

A

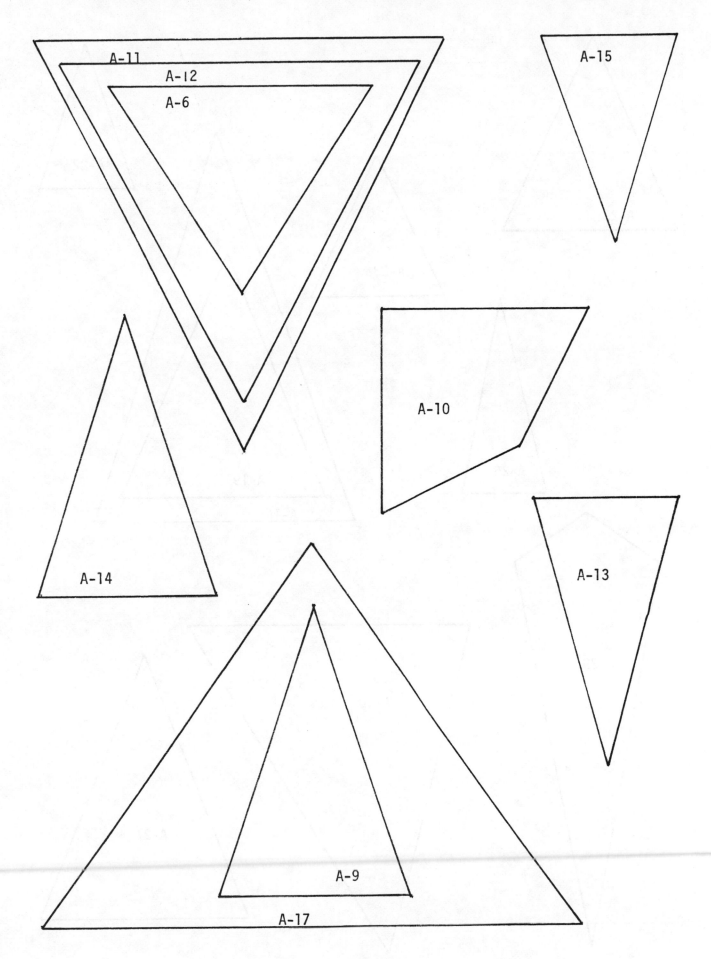

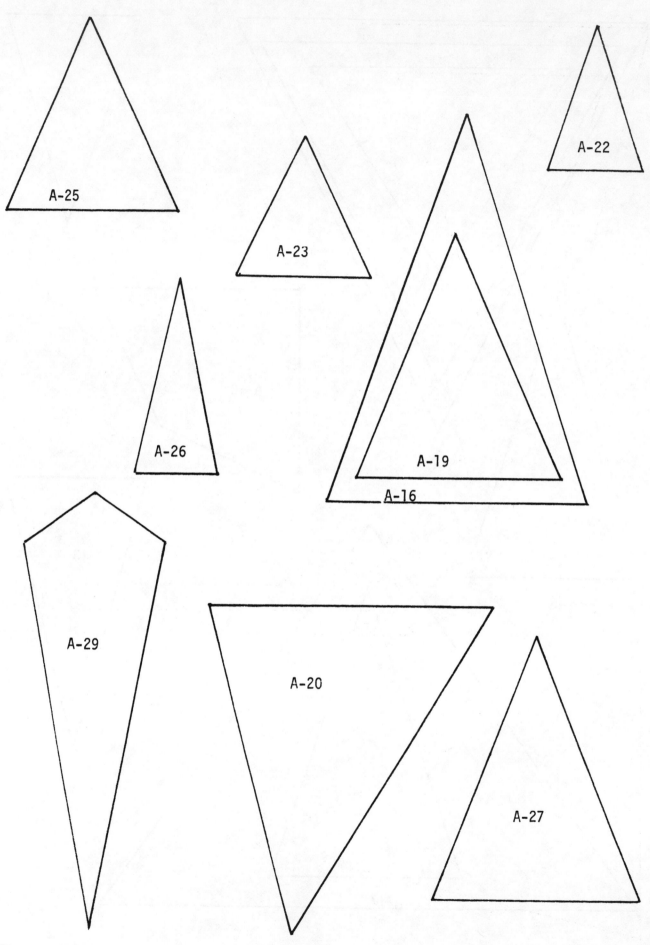

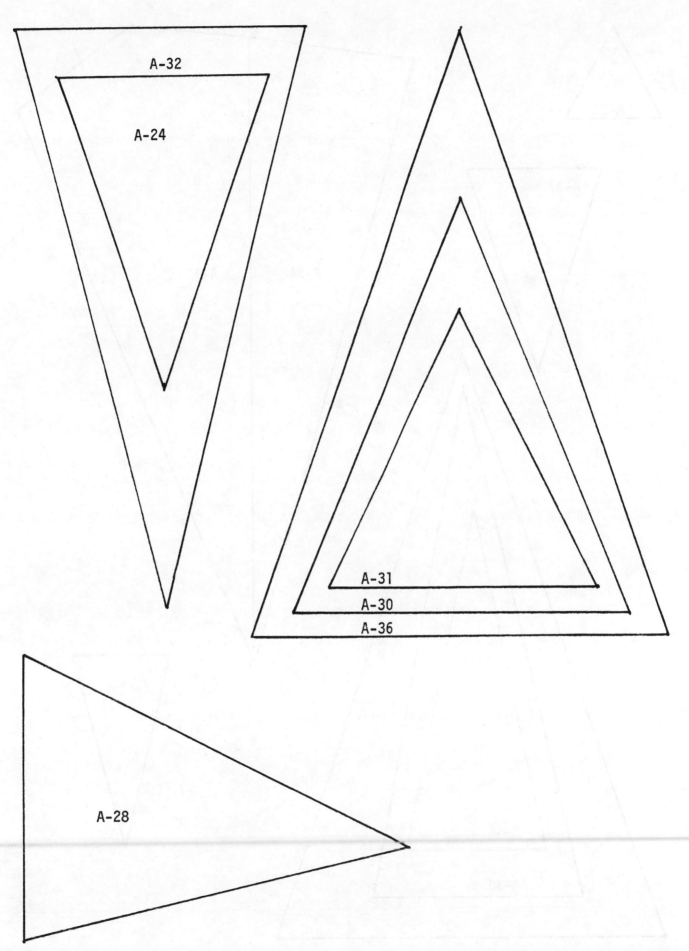

A-32

A-24

A-31
A-30
A-36

A-28

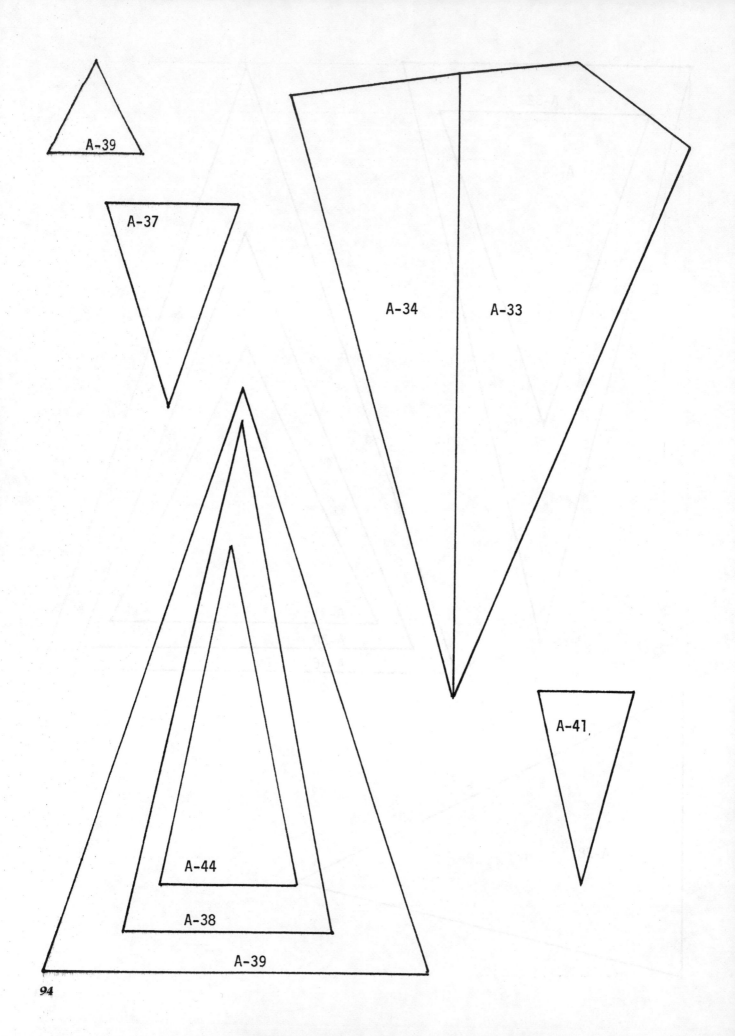

A-39

A-37

A-34

A-33

A-41

A-44

A-38

A-39

94

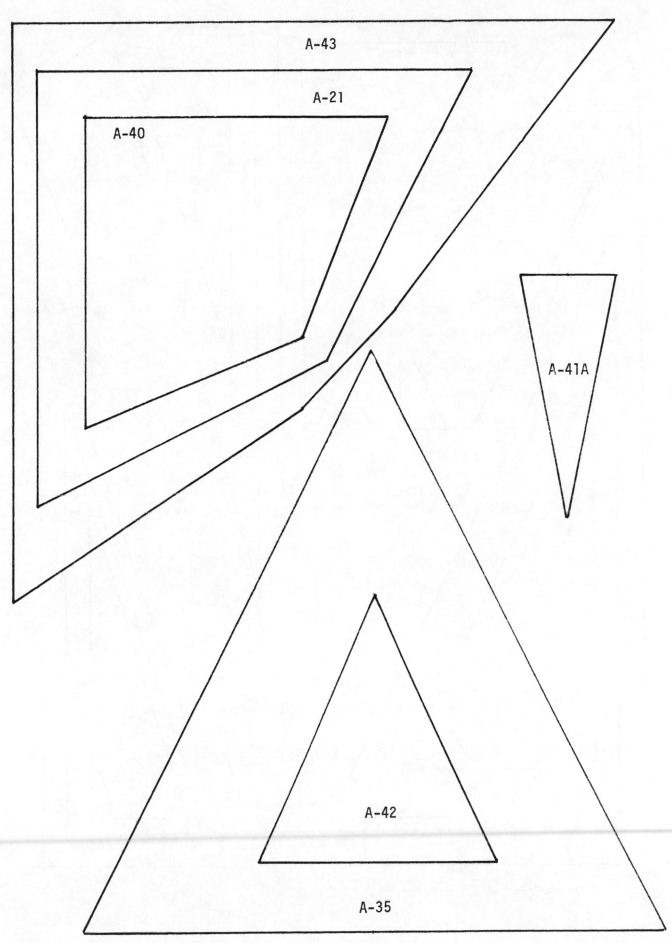

A-43

A-21

A-40

A-41A

A-42

A-35

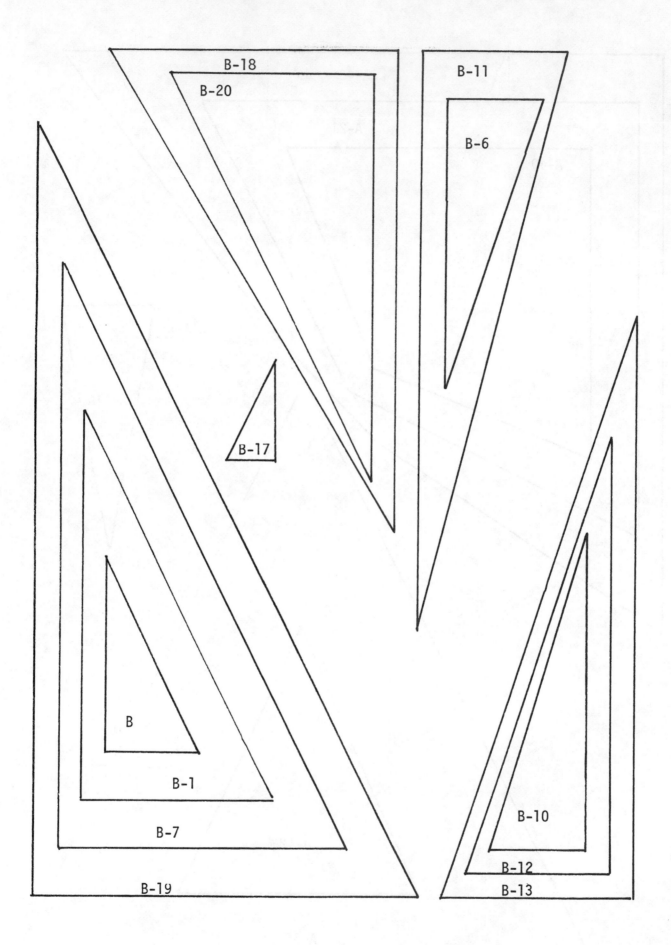

B-18
B-20
B-11
B-6
B-17
B
B-1
B-7
B-10
B-12
B-13
B-19

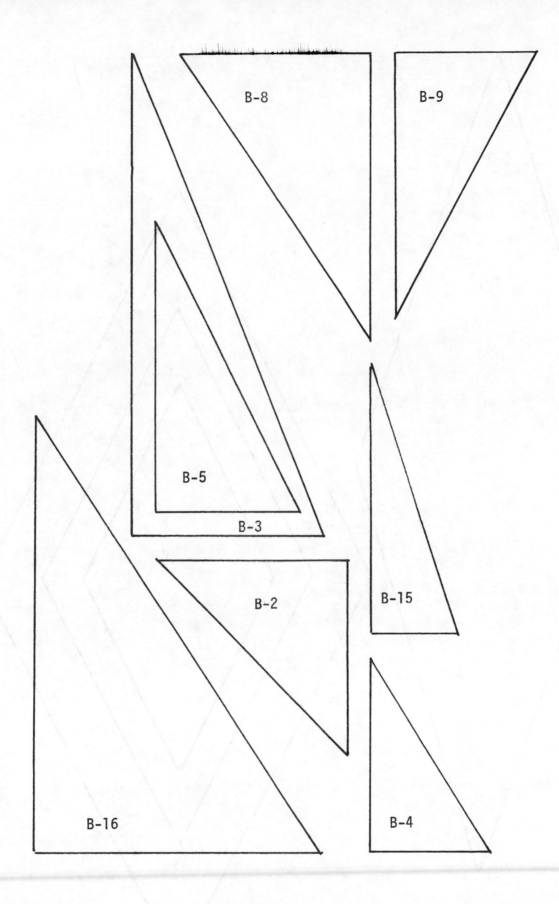

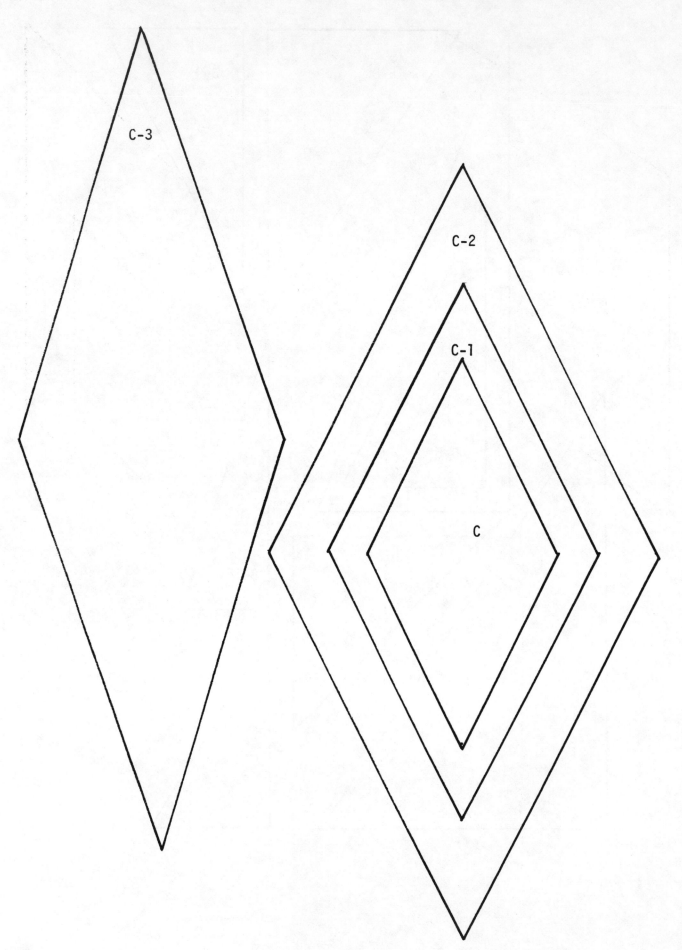

C-3

C-2

C-1

C

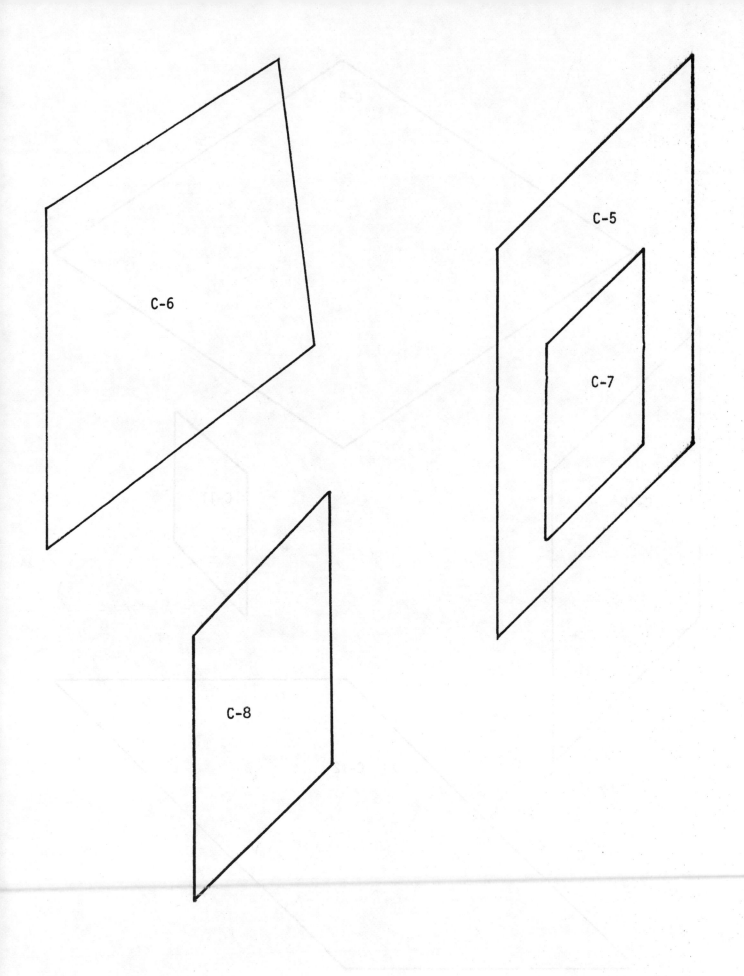

C-6

C-5

C-7

C-8

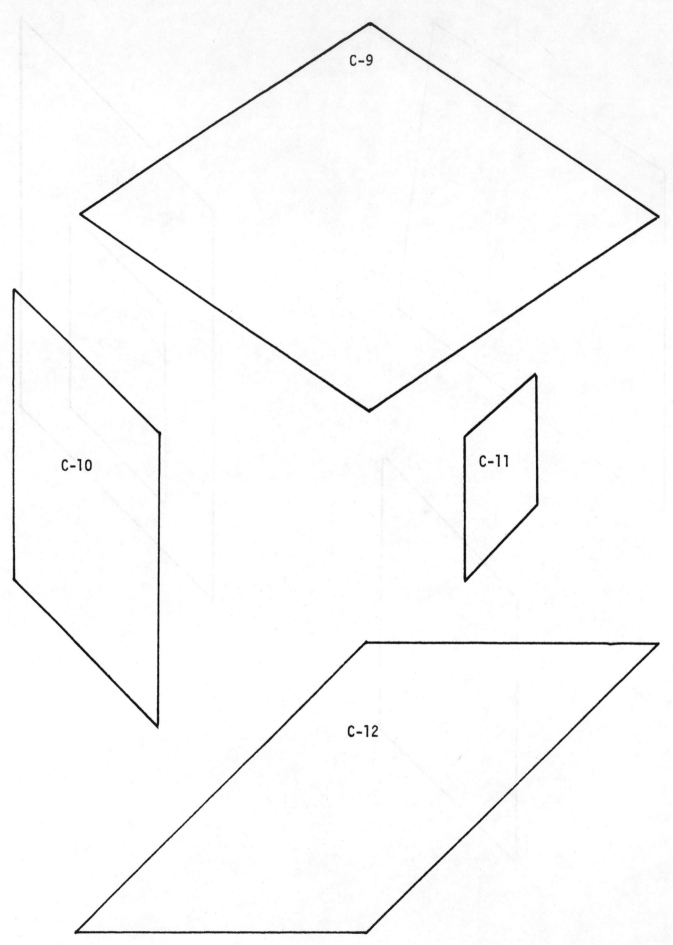

C-9

C-10

C-11

C-12

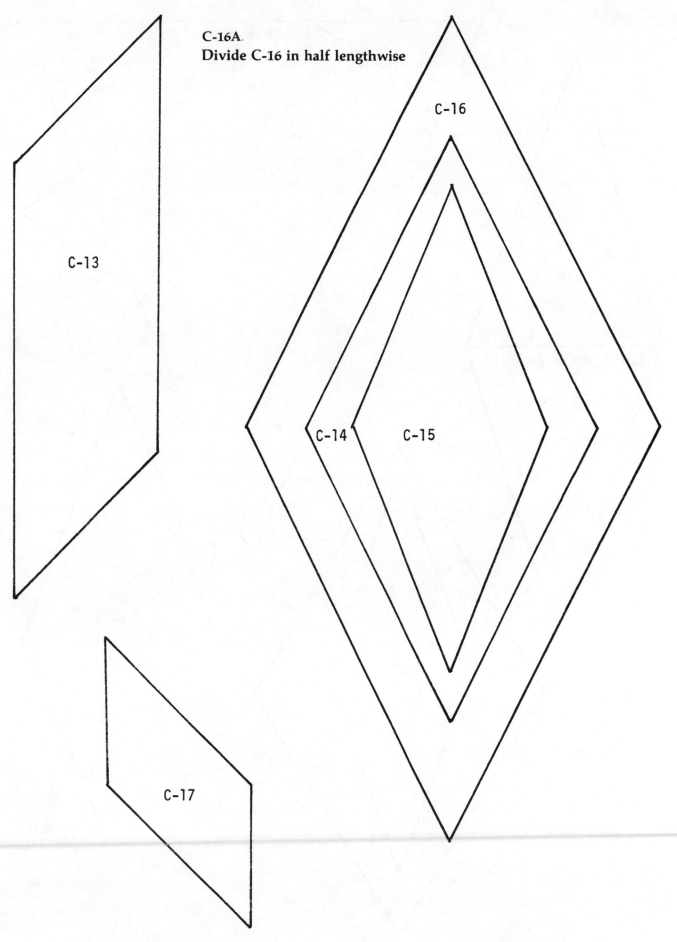

C-16A.
Divide C-16 in half lengthwise

C-16

C-13

C-14   C-15

C-17

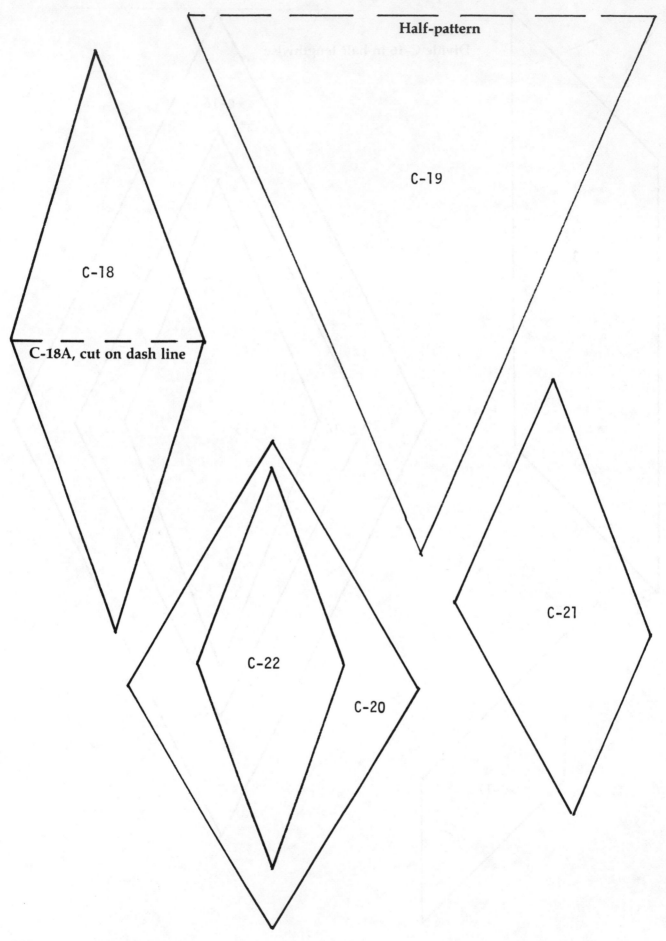

Half-pattern

C-19

C-18

C-18A, cut on dash line

C-22

C-20

C-21

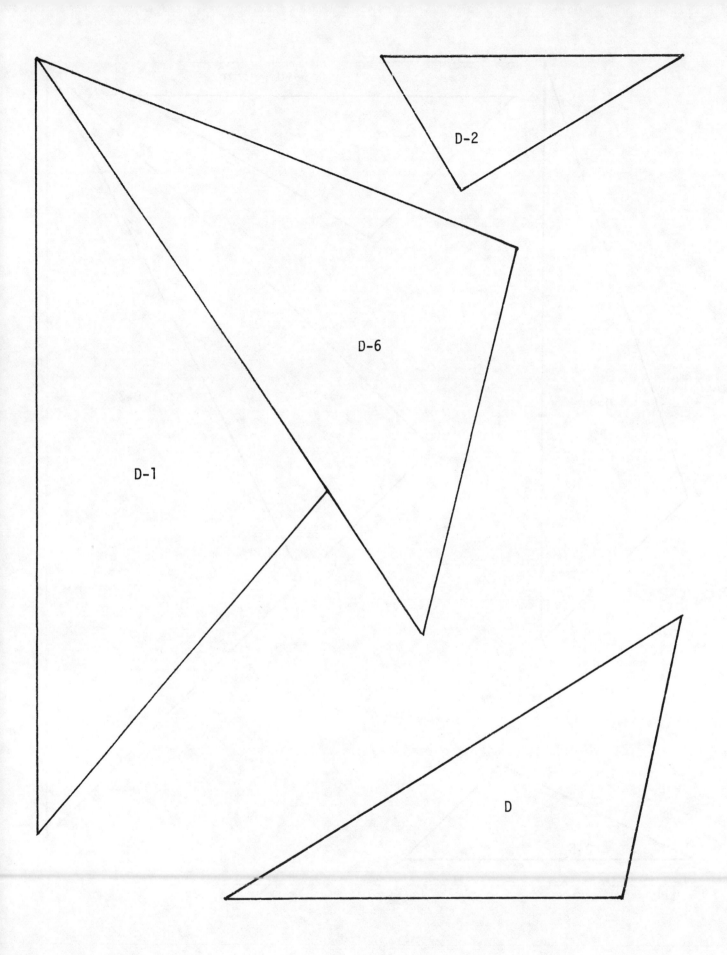

D-2

D-6

D-1

D

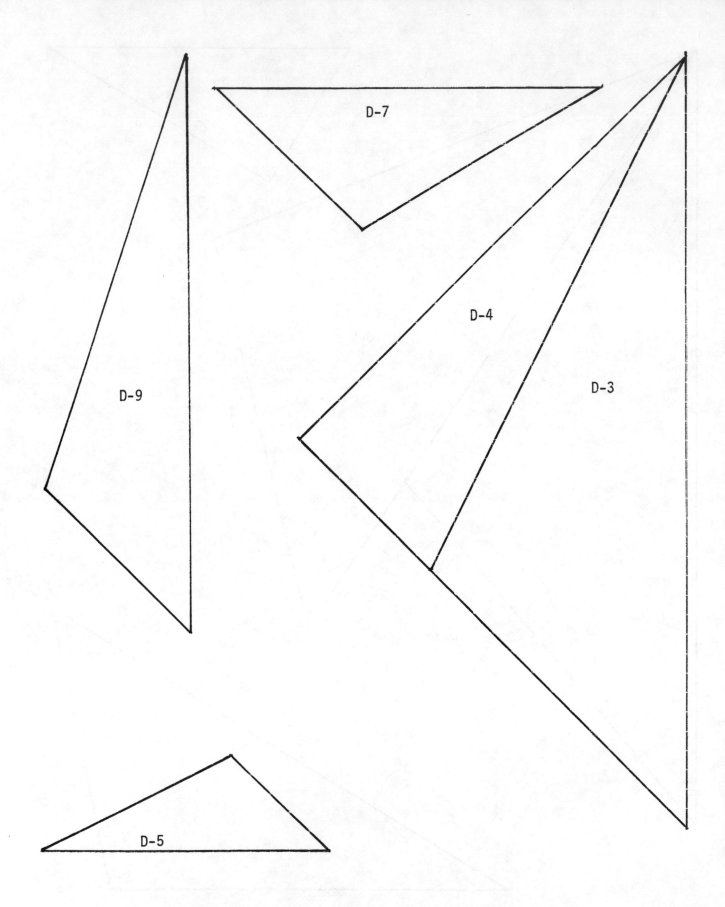

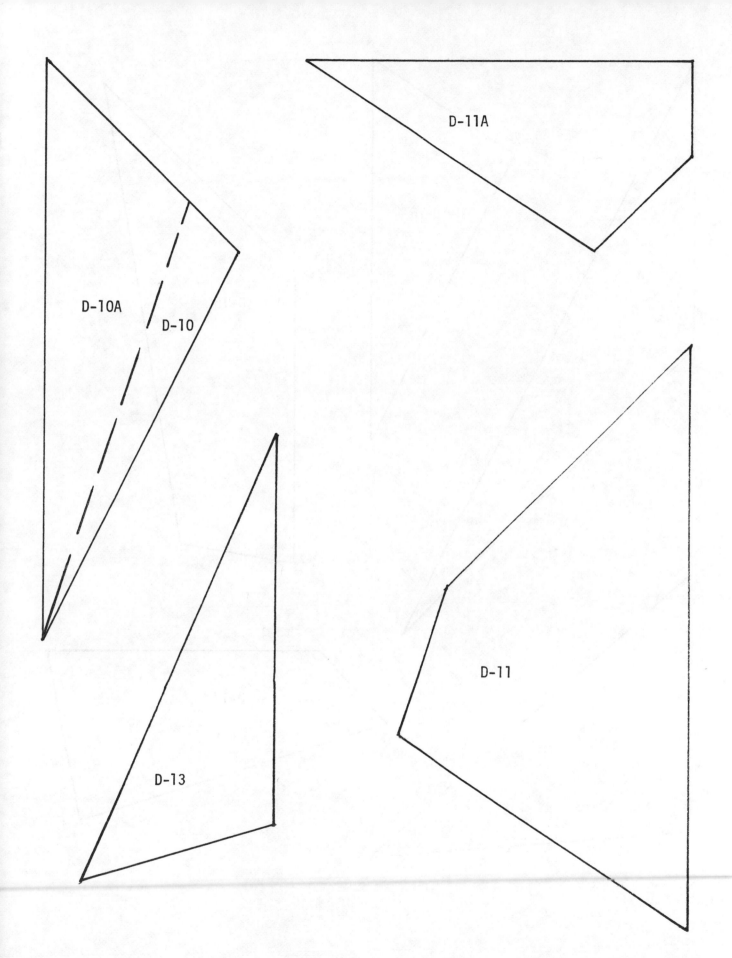

D-11A

D-10A

D-10

D-13

D-11

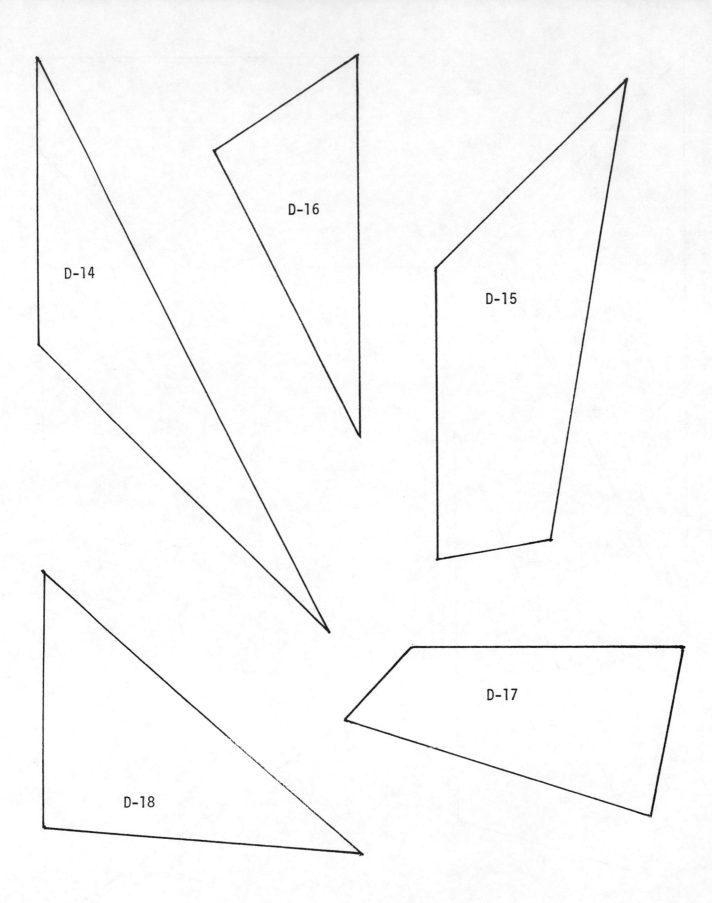

D-16

D-14

D-15

D-18

D-17

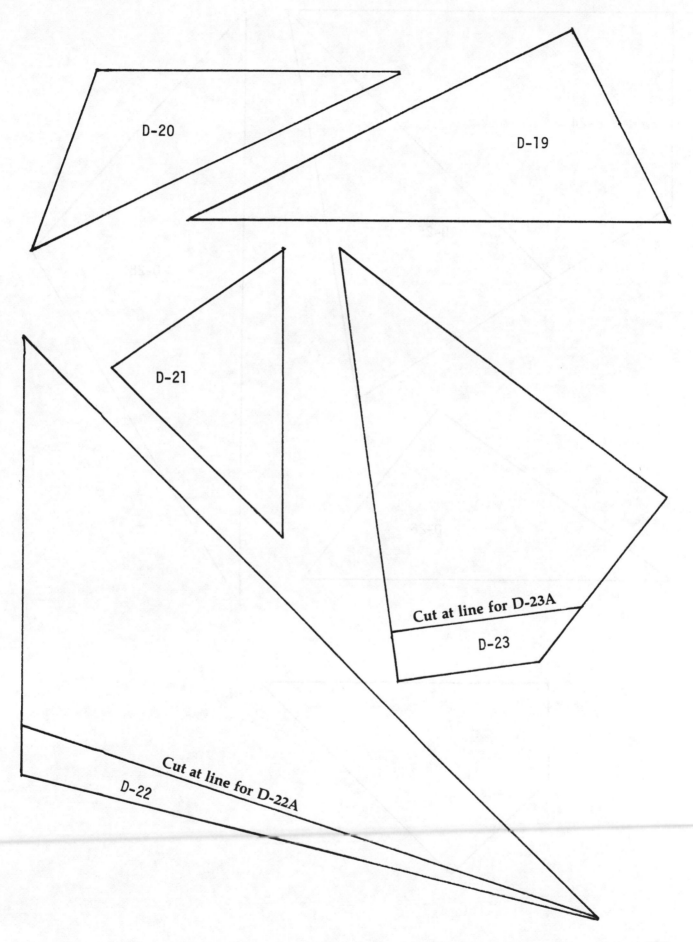

D-20

D-19

D-21

Cut at line for D-23A

D-23

Cut at line for D-22A

D-22

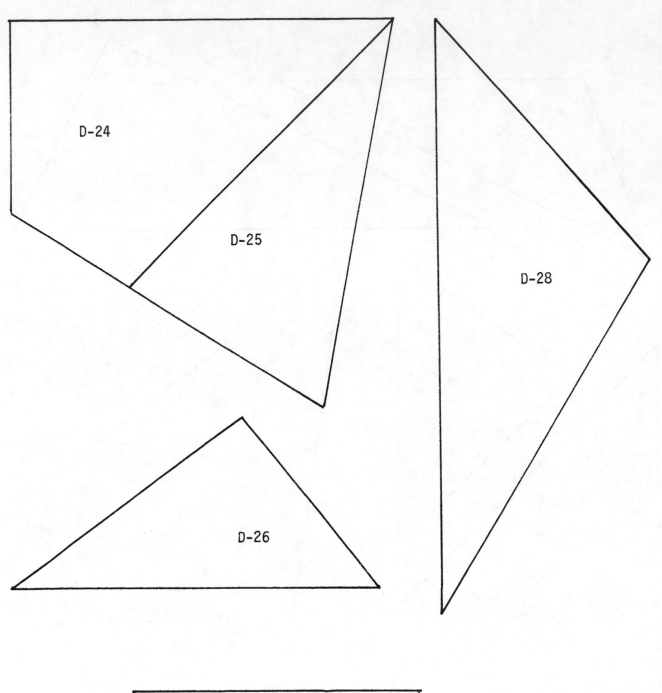

D-24

D-25

D-26

D-28

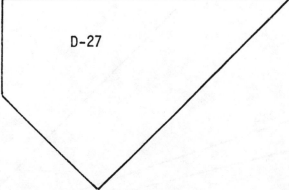

D-27

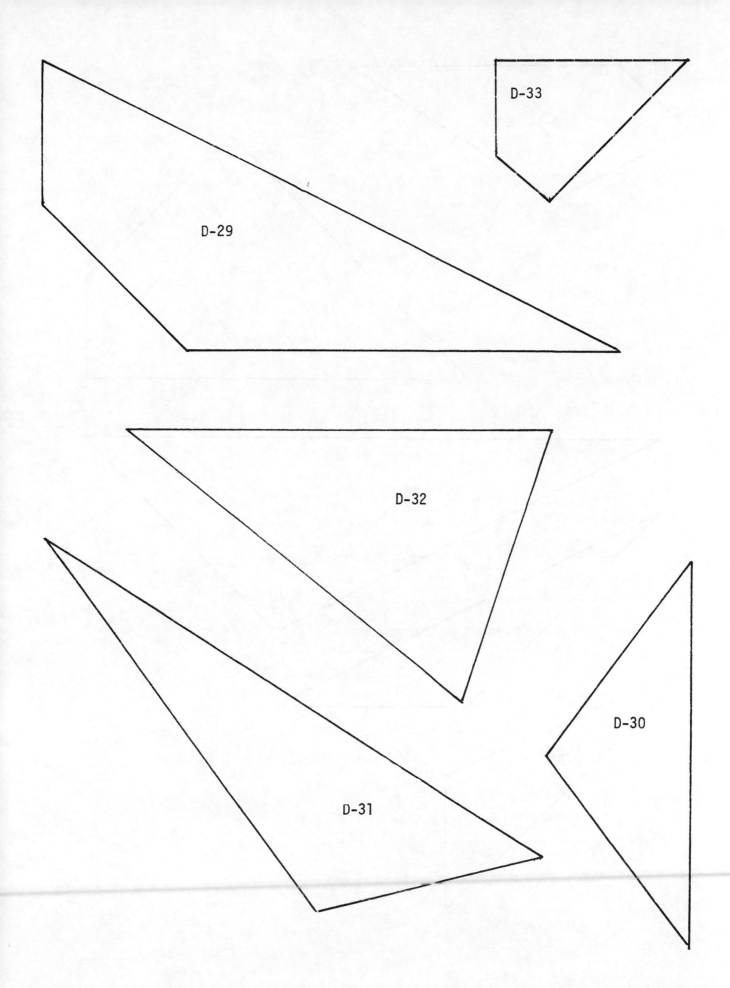

D-33

D-29

D-32

D-31

D-30

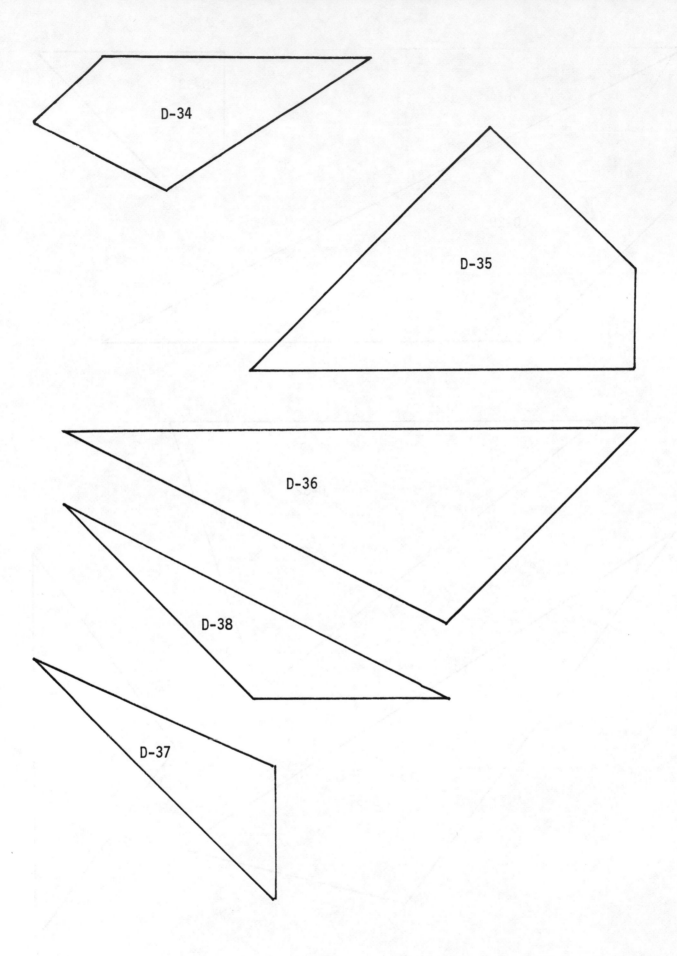

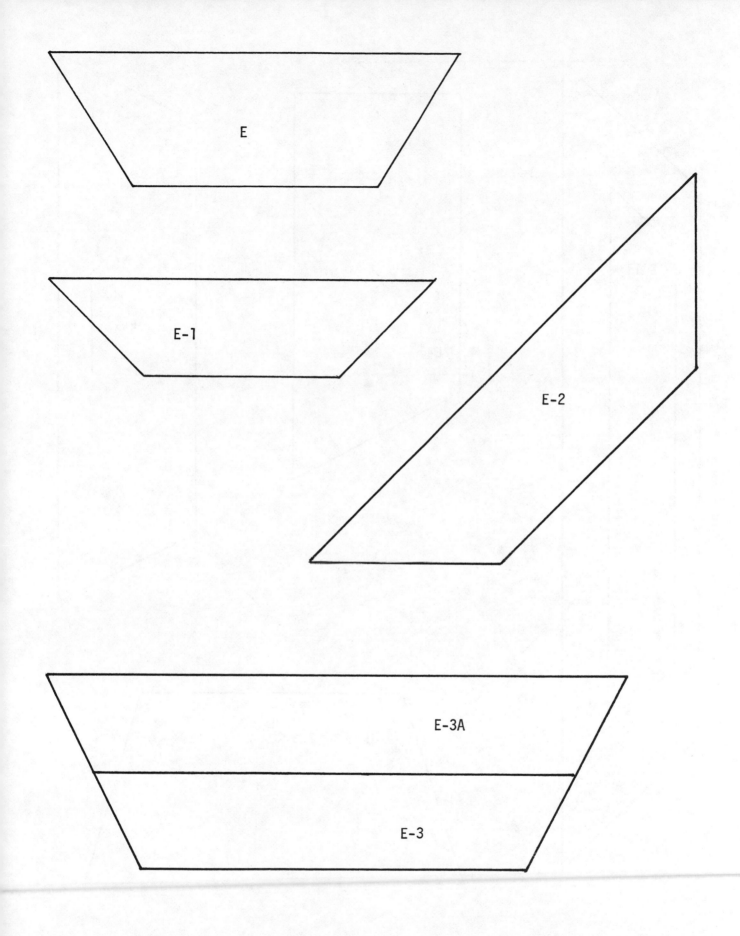

E

E-1

E-2

E-3A

E-3

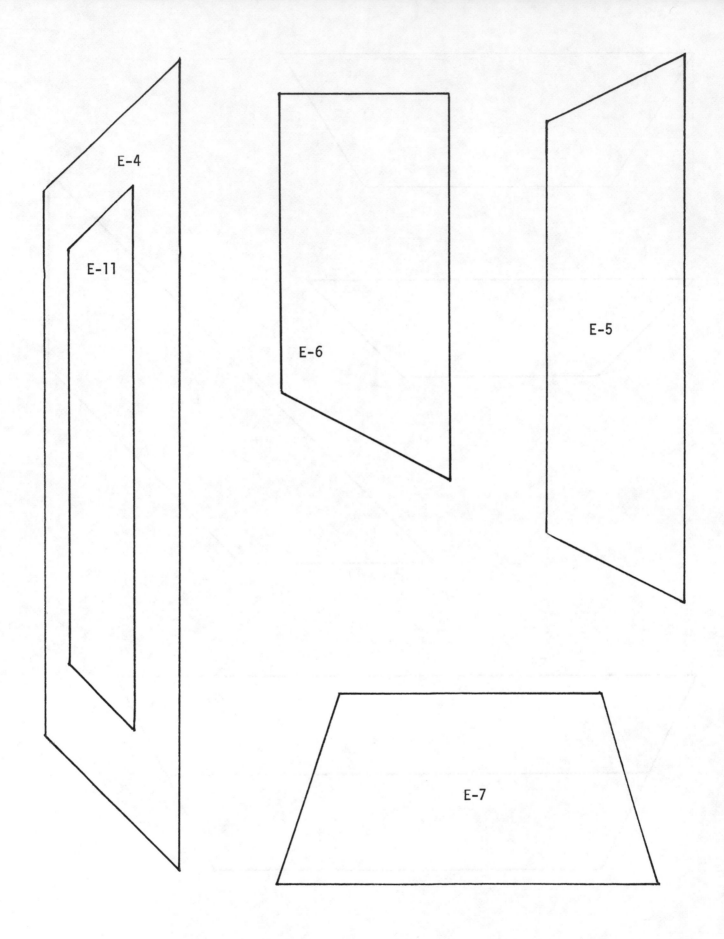

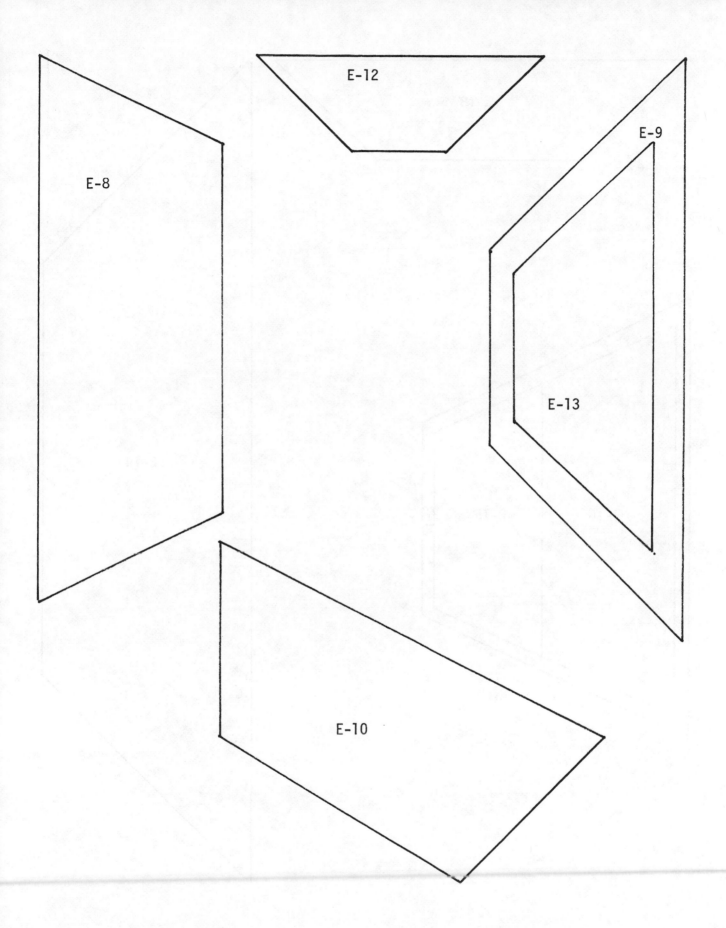

E-12

E-9

E-8

E-13

E-10

113

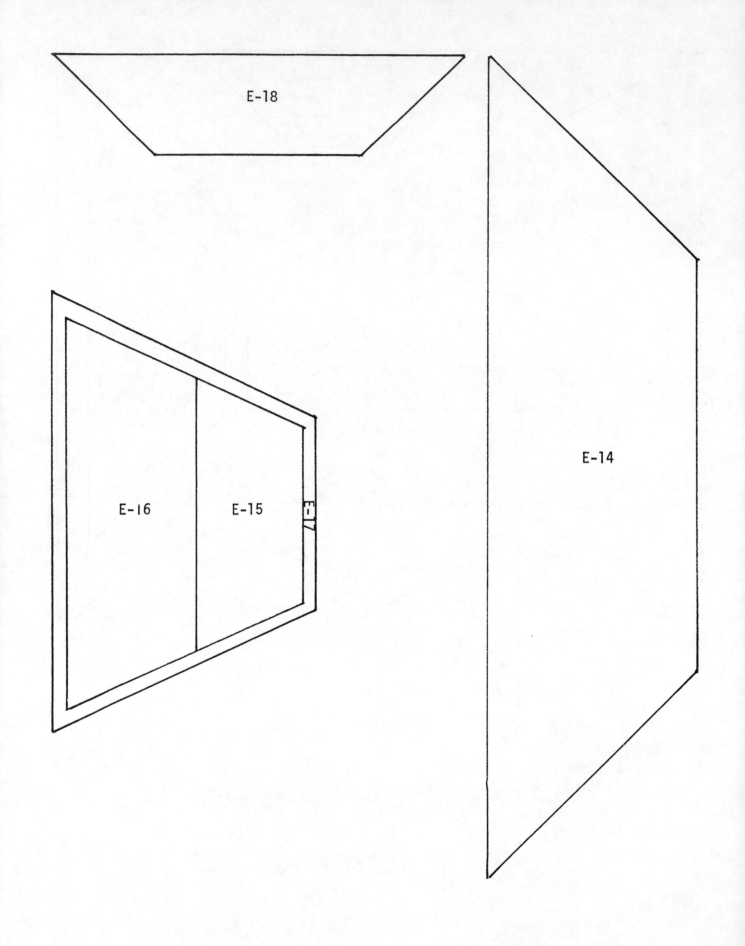

E-18

E-14

E-16

E-15

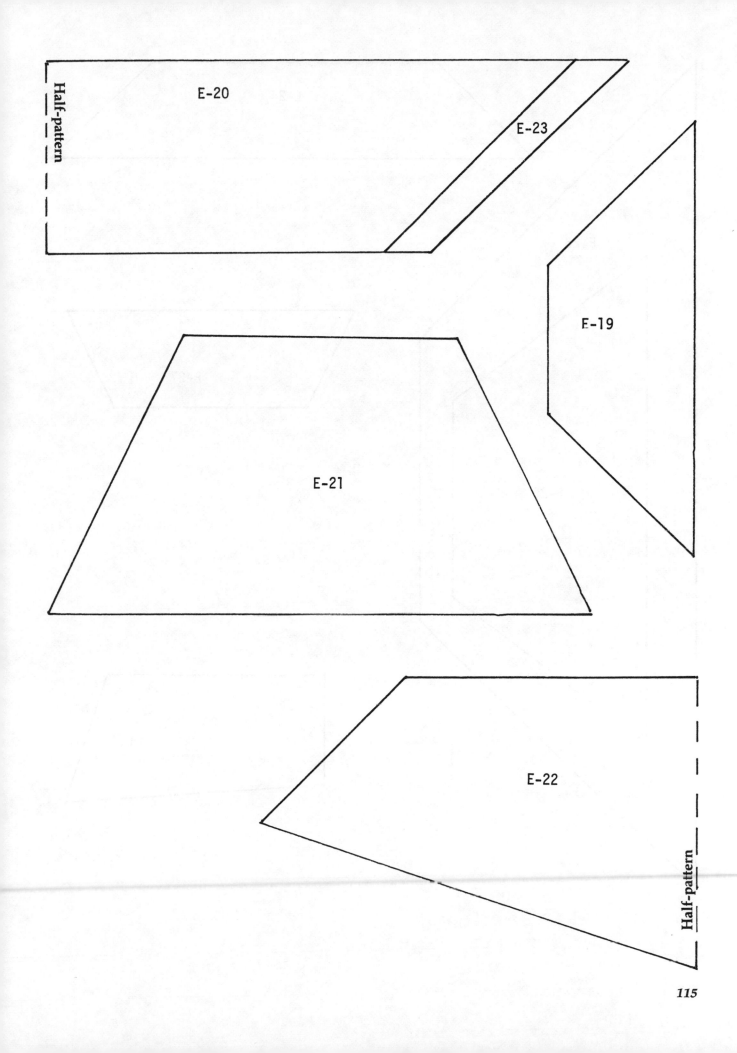

E-20

Half-pattern

E-23

E-19

E-21

E-22

Half-pattern

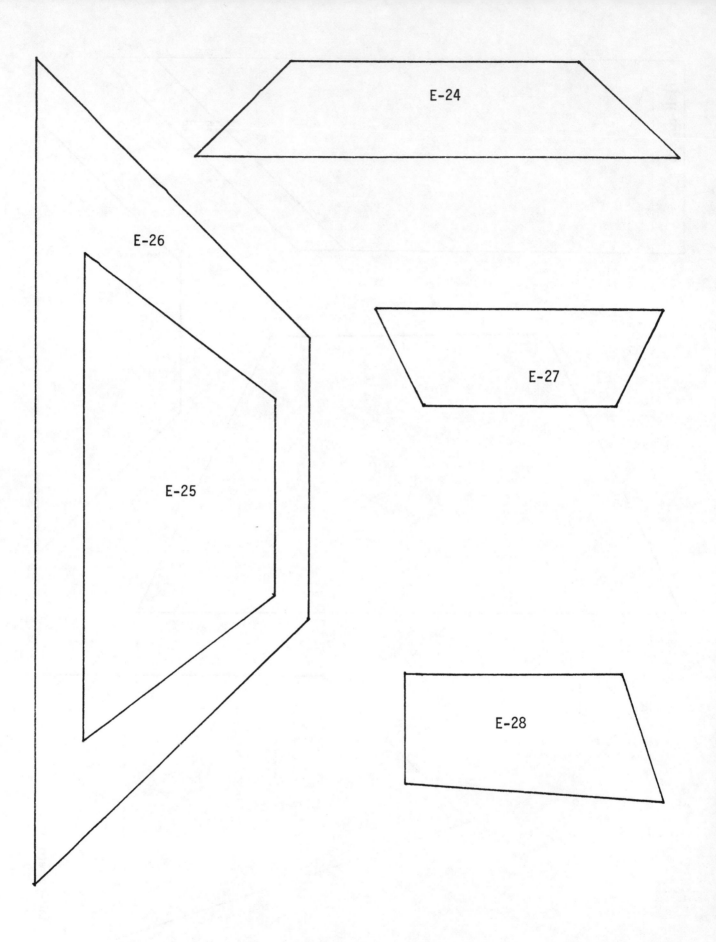

E-24

E-26

E-27

E-25

E-28

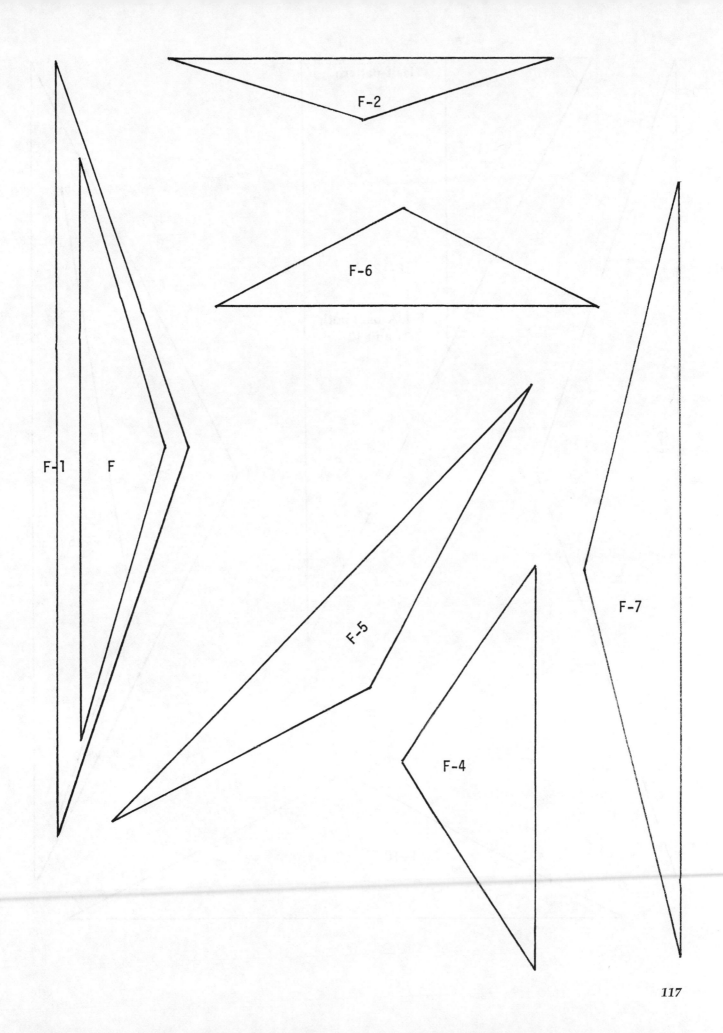

F-2

F-6

F-1 F

F-5

F-7

F-4

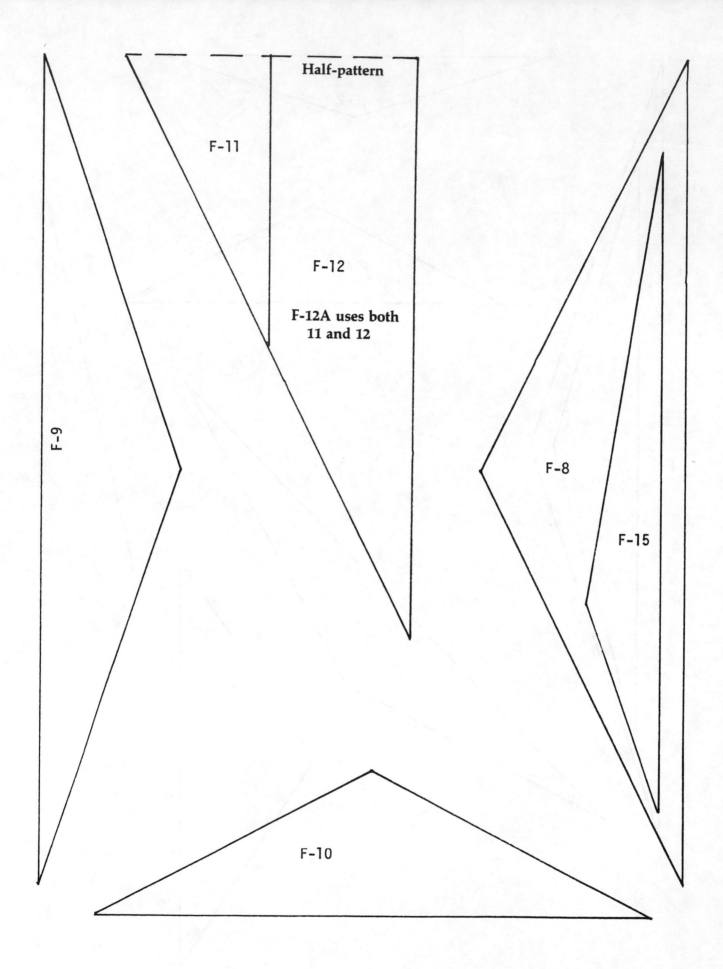

Half-pattern

F-11

F-12

F-12A uses both
11 and 12

F-9

F-8

F-15

F-10

118

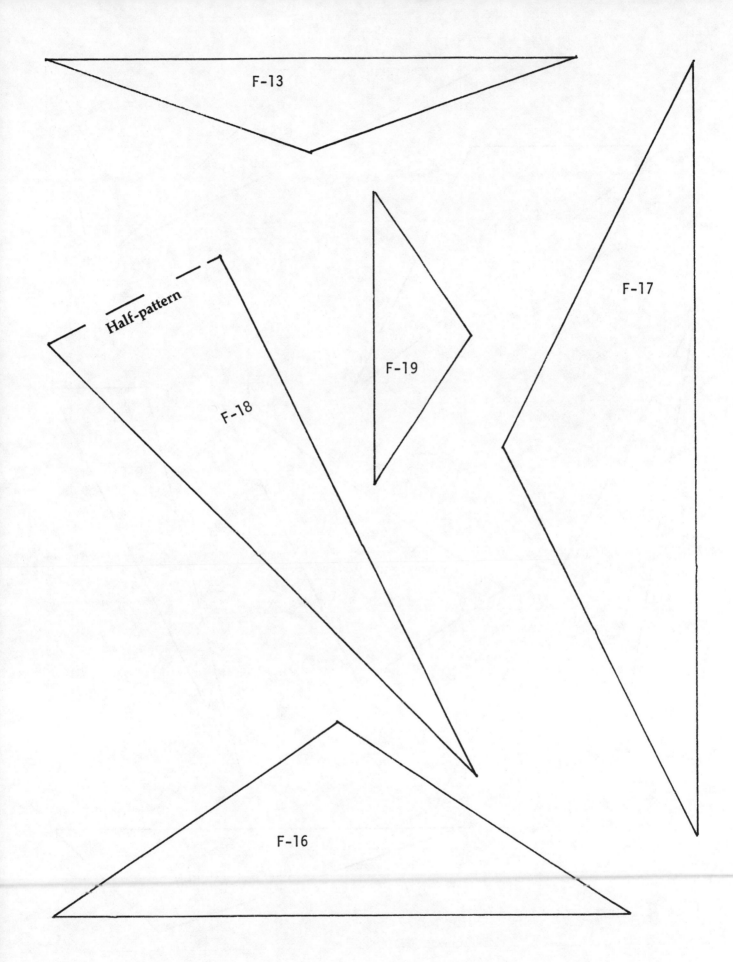

F-13

Half-pattern

F-18

F-19

F-17

F-16

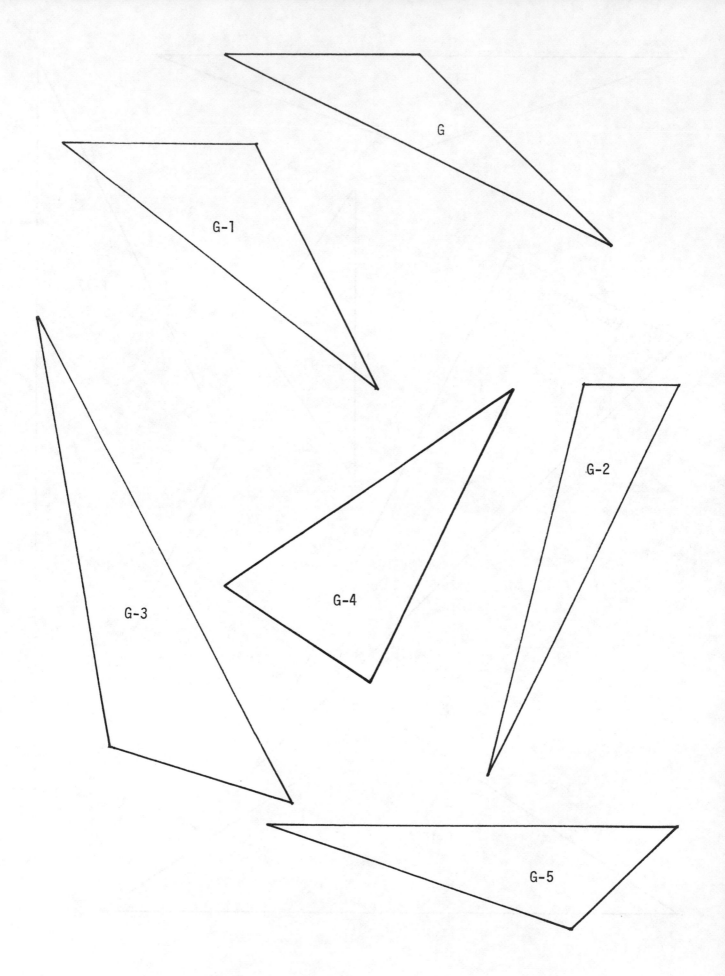

G

G-1

G-2

G-3

G-4

G-5

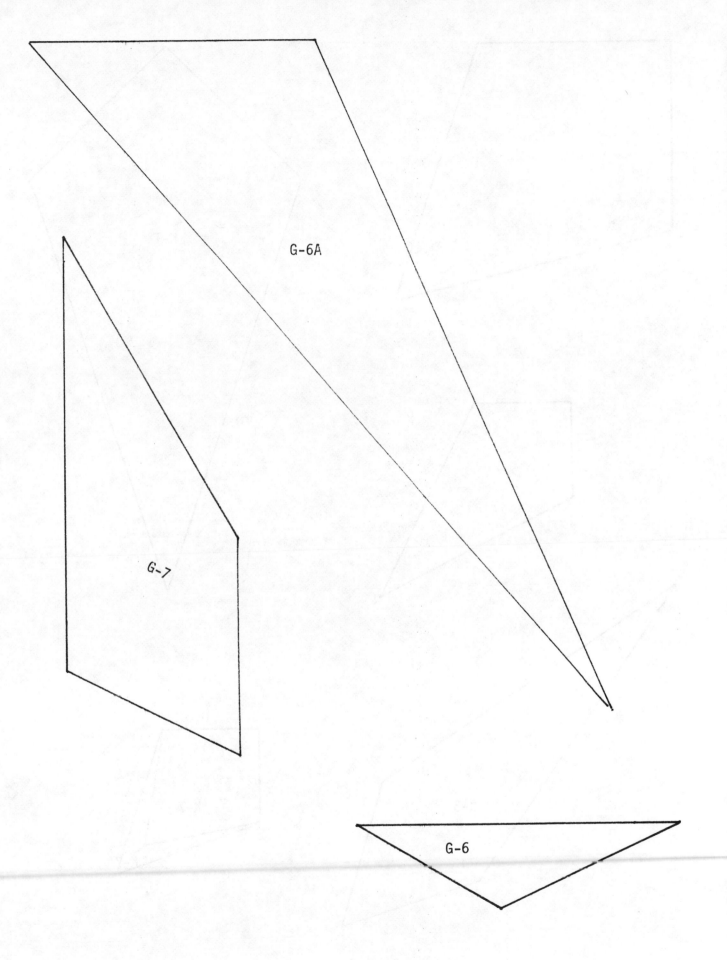

G-6A

G-7

G-6

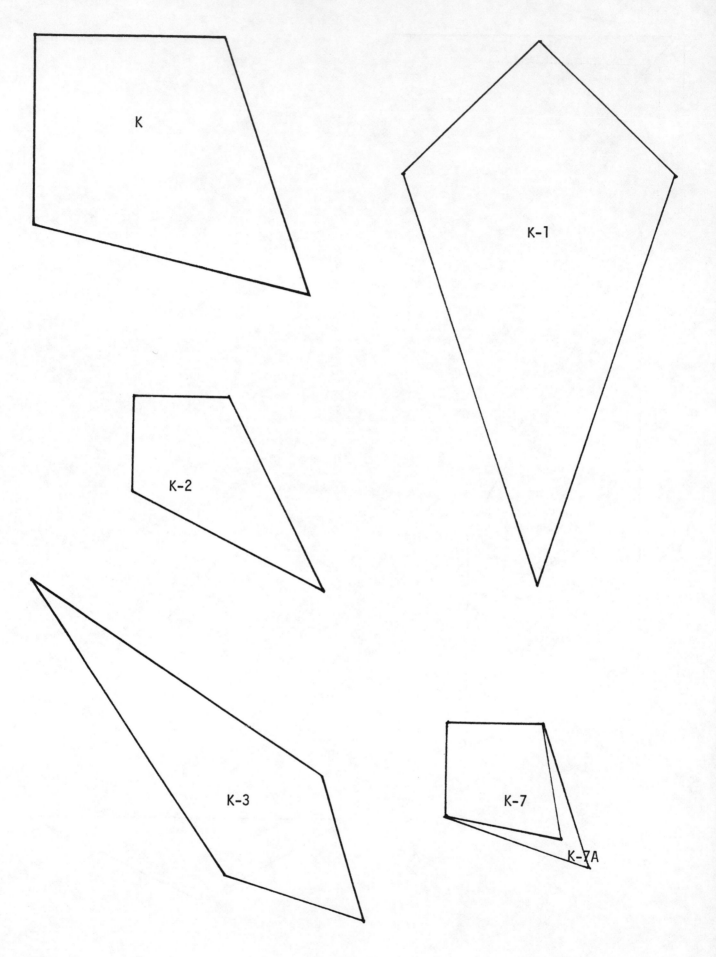

K

K-1

K-2

K-3

K-7

K-7A

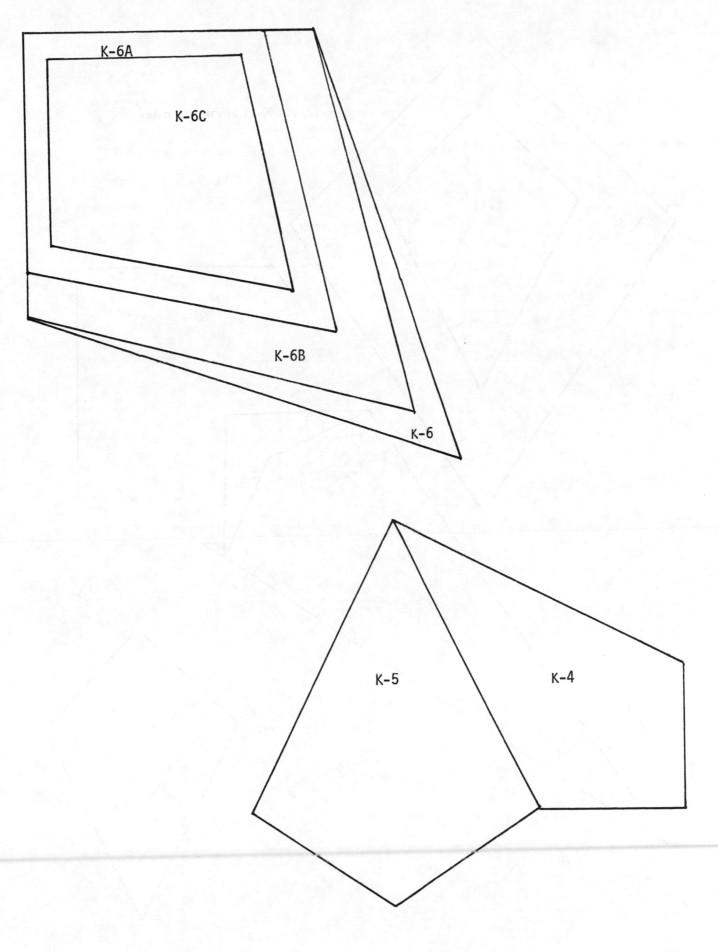

K-6A

K-6C

K-6B

K-6

K-5

K-4

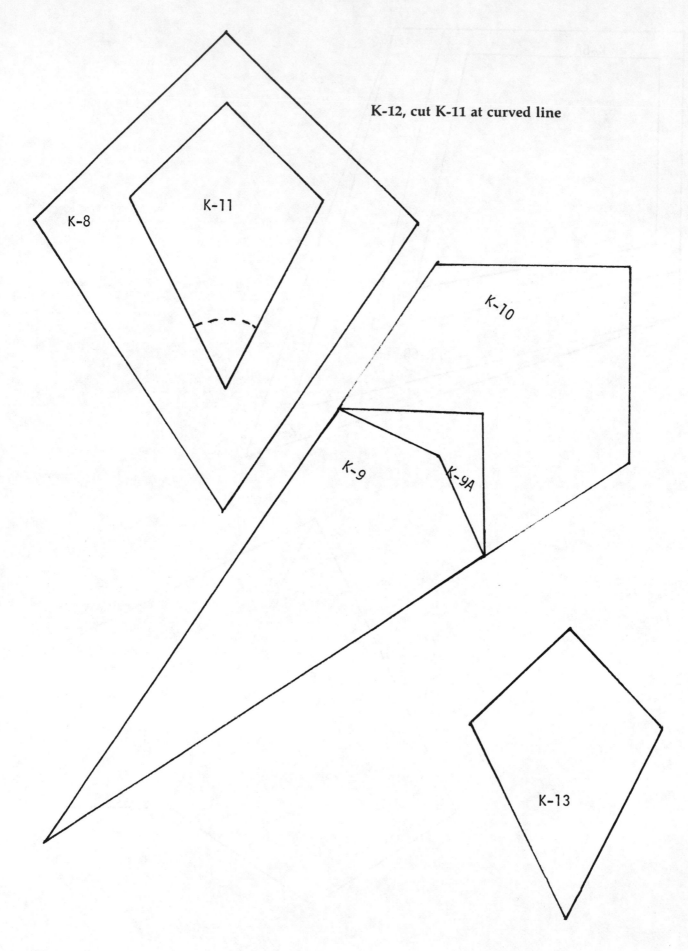

K-12, cut K-11 at curved line

K-11

K-8

K-10

K-9

K-9A

K-13

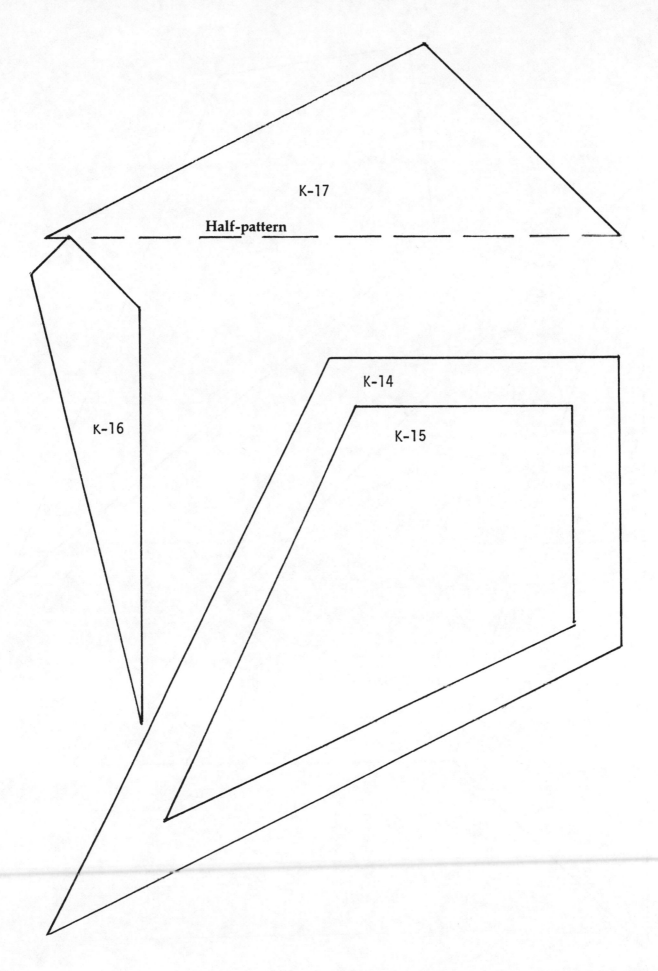

K-17

Half-pattern

K-16

K-14

K-15

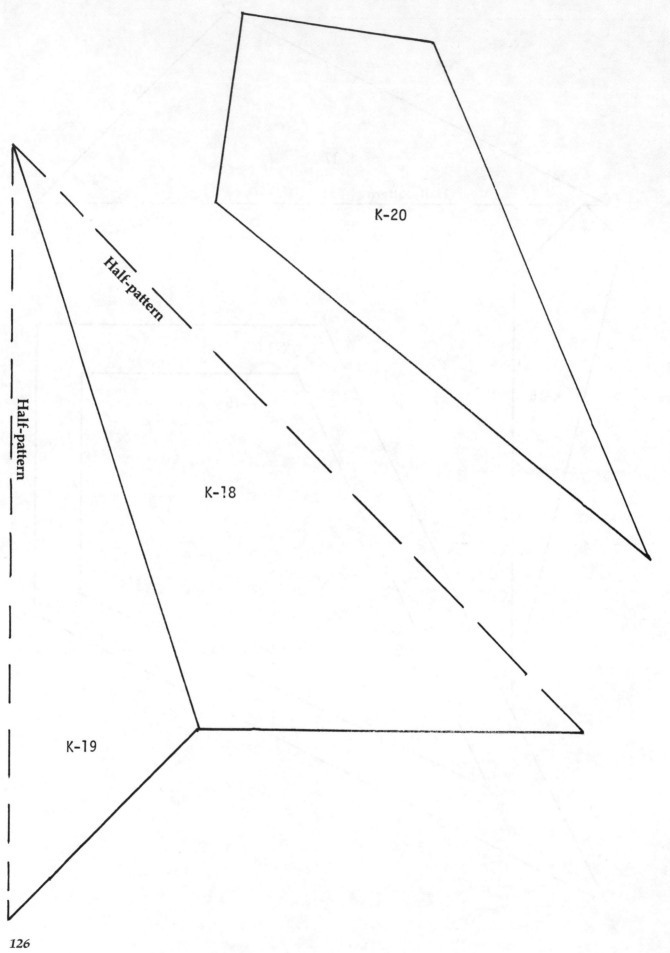

K-20

Half-pattern

Half-pattern

K-18

K-19

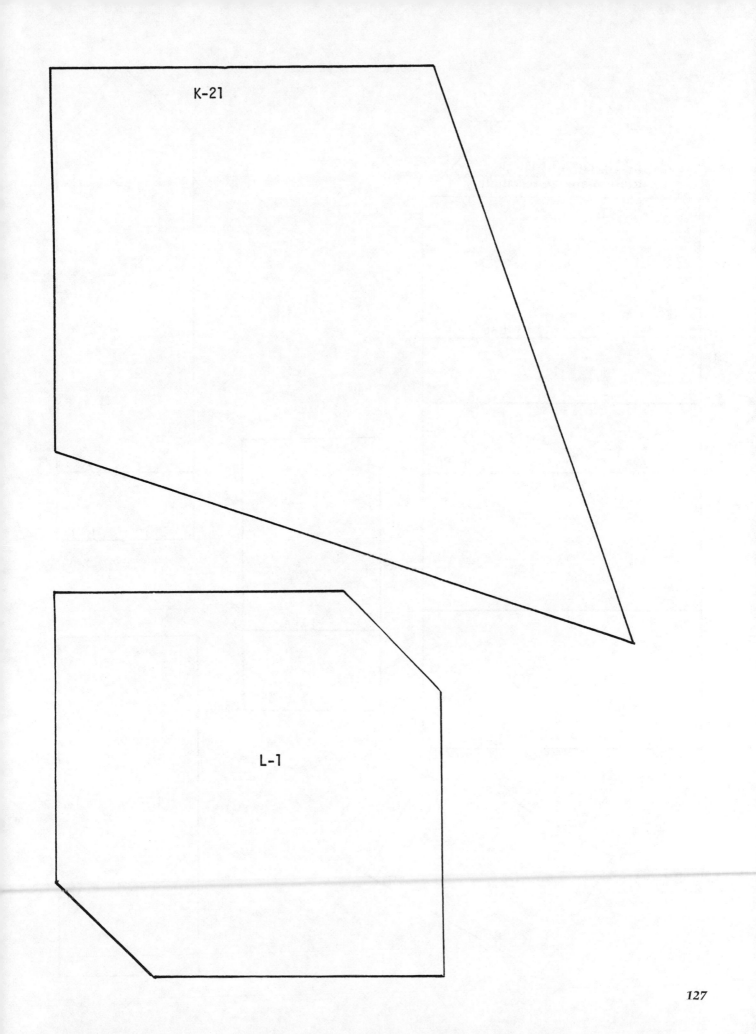

K-21

L-1

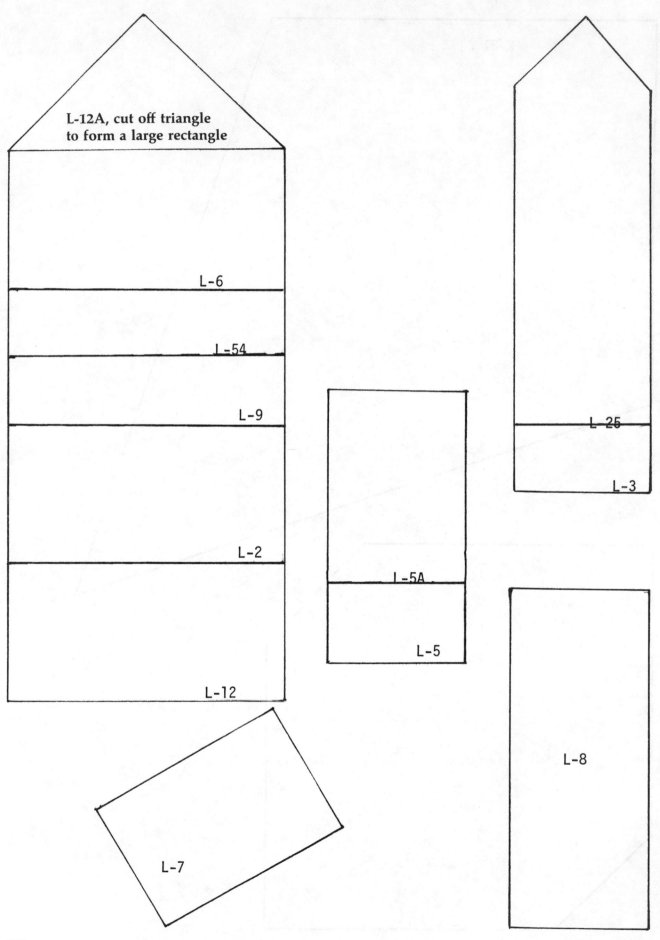

L-12A, cut off triangle
to form a large rectangle

L-6

L-54

L-9

L-2

L-12

L-7

L-5A

L-5

L-25

L-3

L-8

128

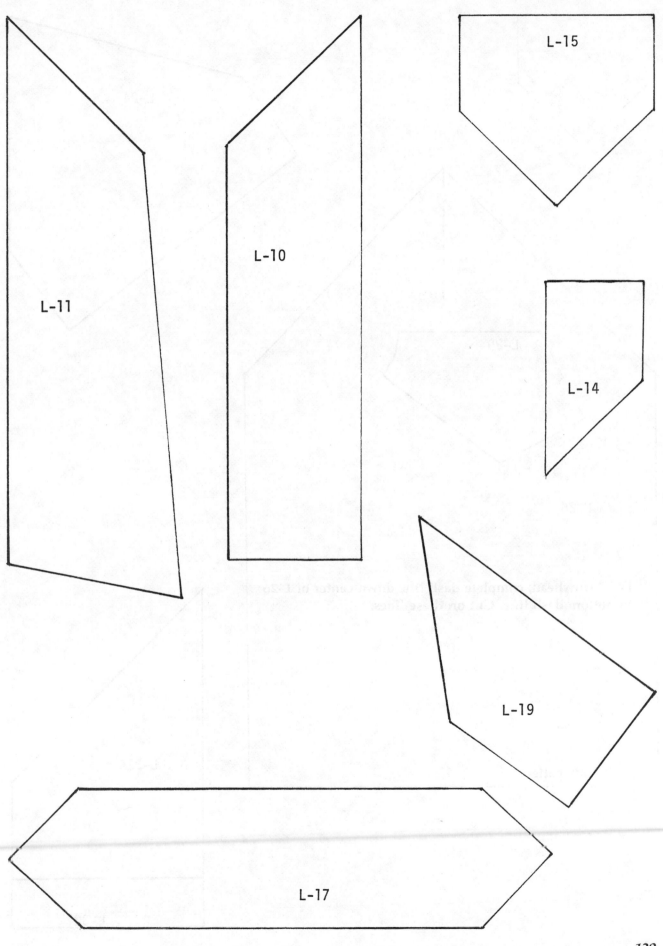

L-15

L-10

L-11

L-14

L-19

L-17

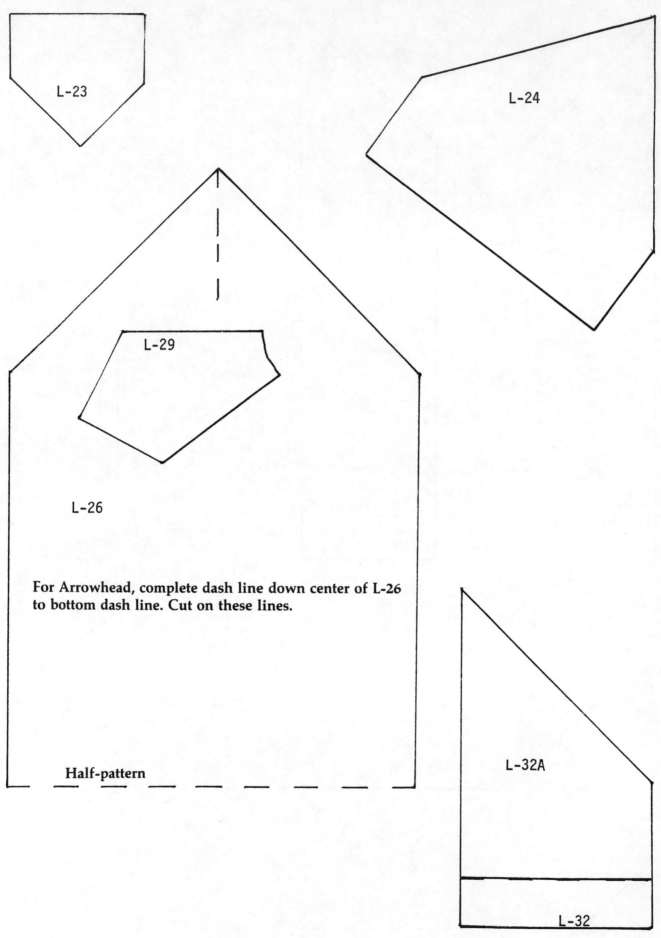

L-23

L-24

L-29

L-26

For Arrowhead, complete dash line down center of L-26 to bottom dash line. Cut on these lines.

Half-pattern

L-32A

L-32

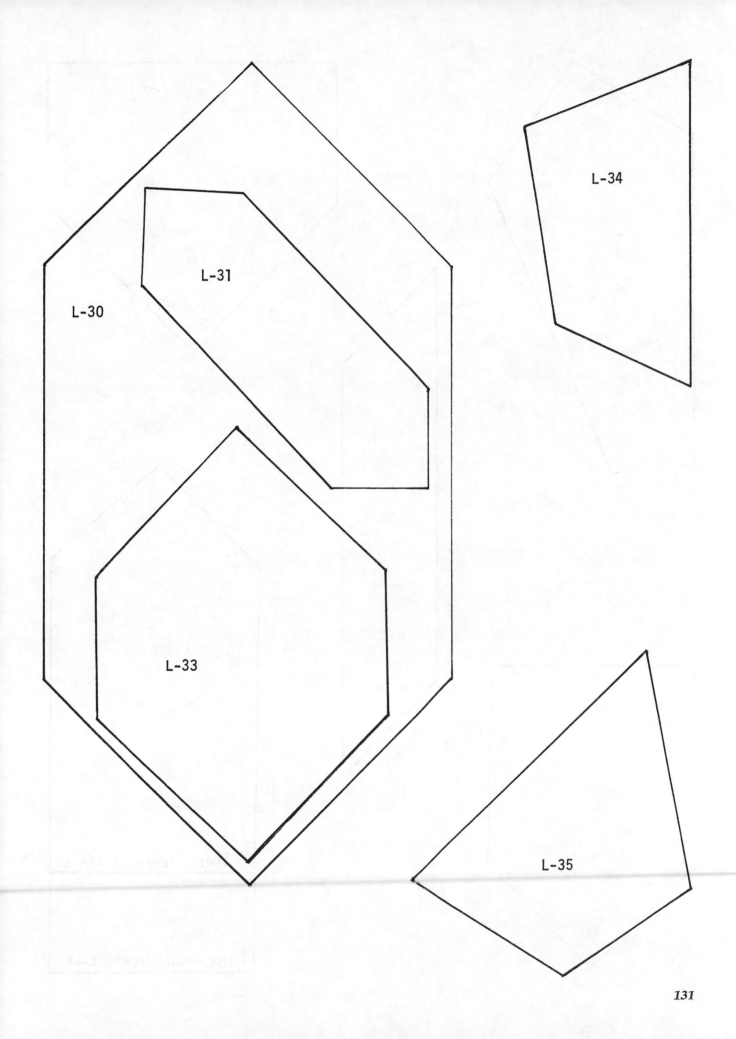

L-34

L-31

L-30

L-33

L-35

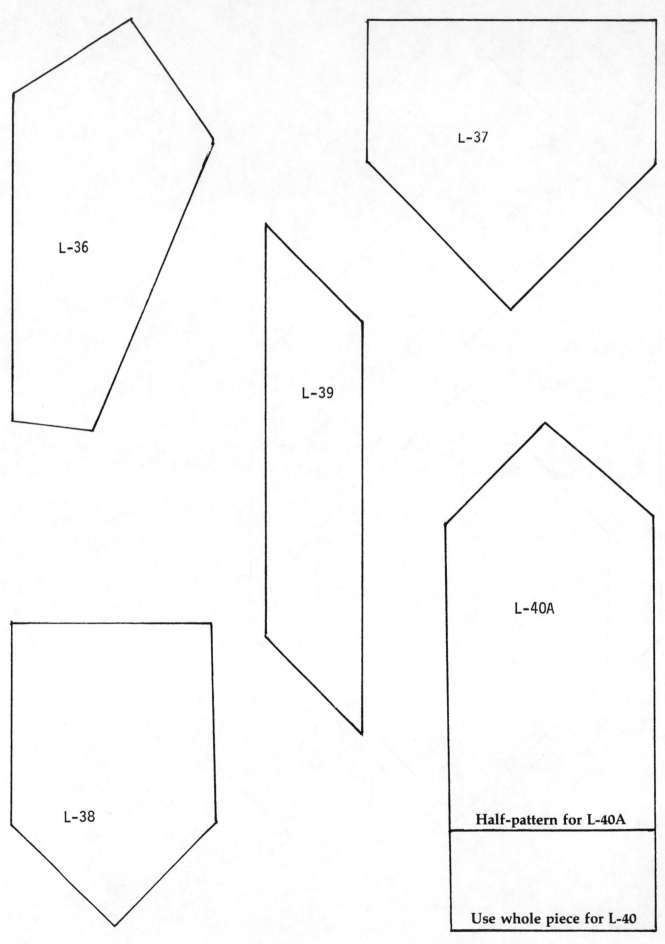

L-36

L-37

L-39

L-38

L-40A

Half-pattern for L-40A

Use whole piece for L-40

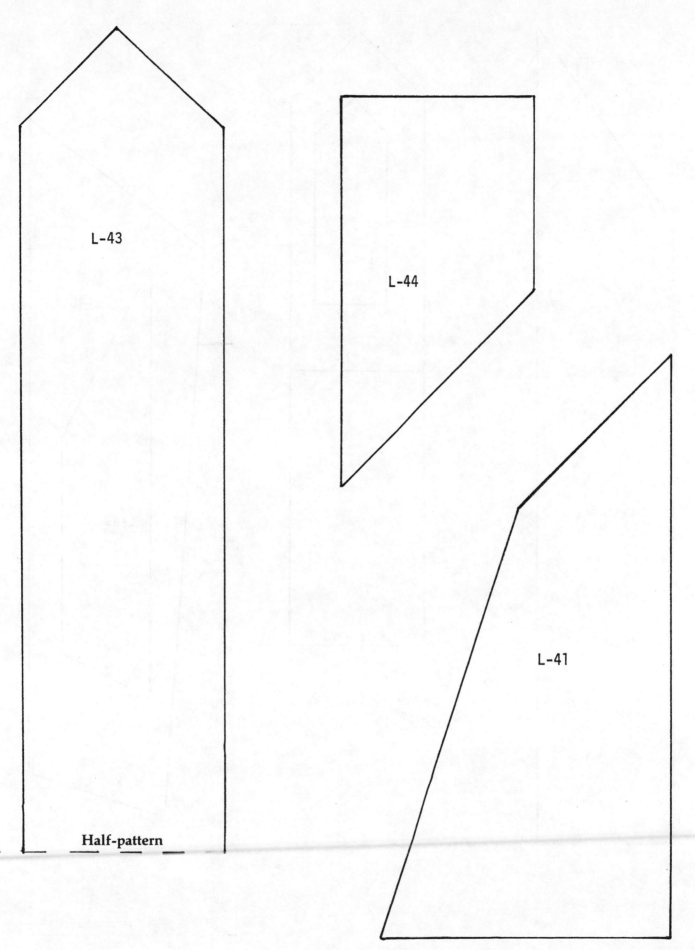

L-43

Half-pattern

L-44

L-41

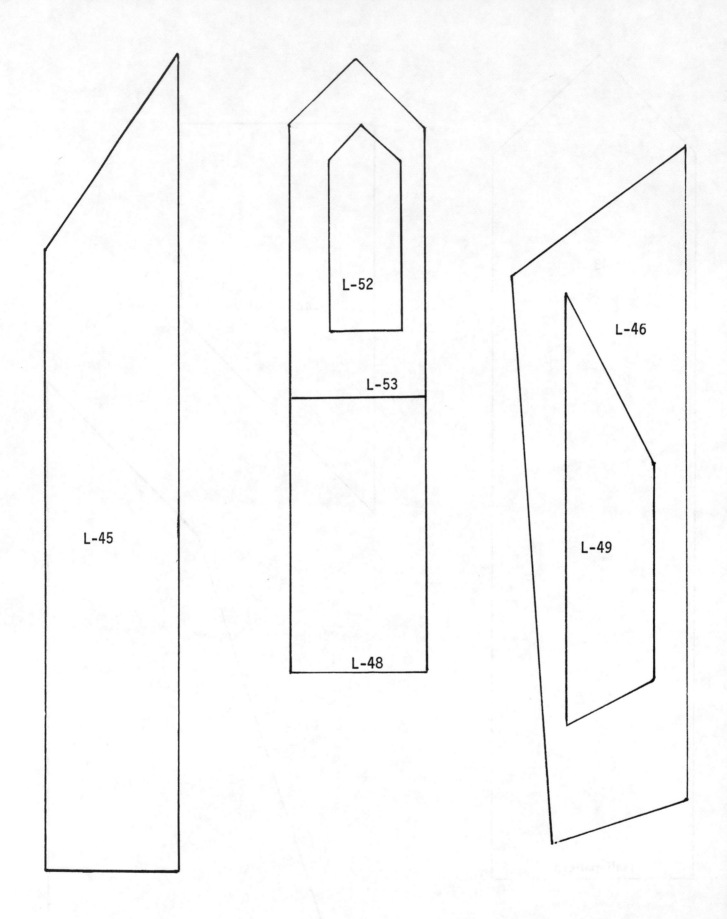

L-45

L-52

L-53

L-48

L-46

L-49

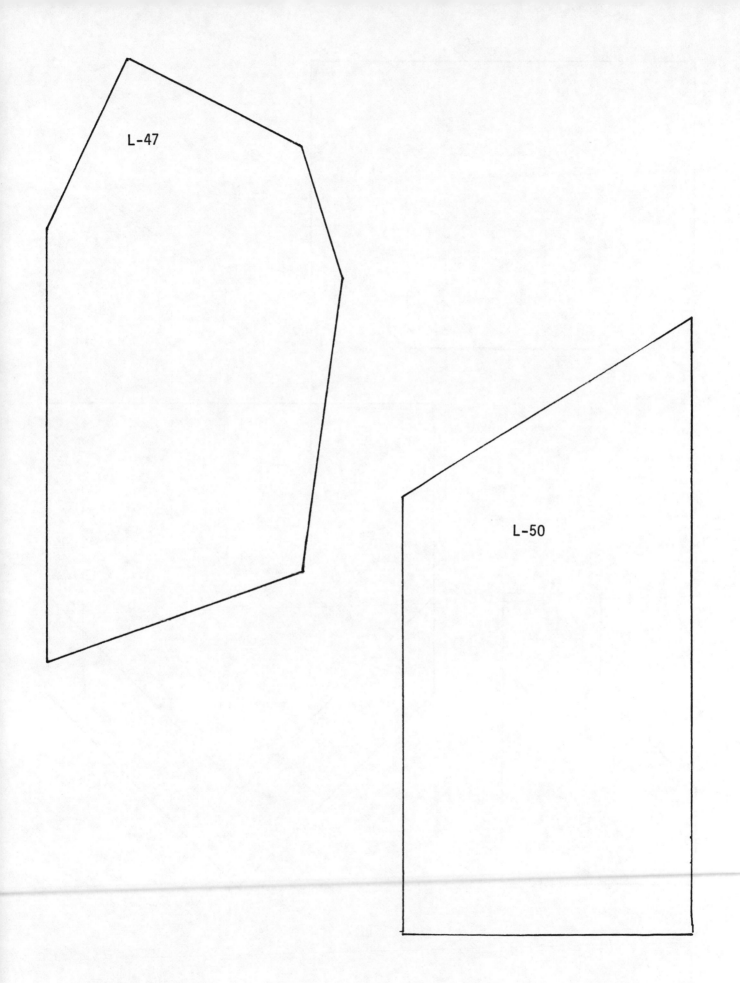

L-47

L-50

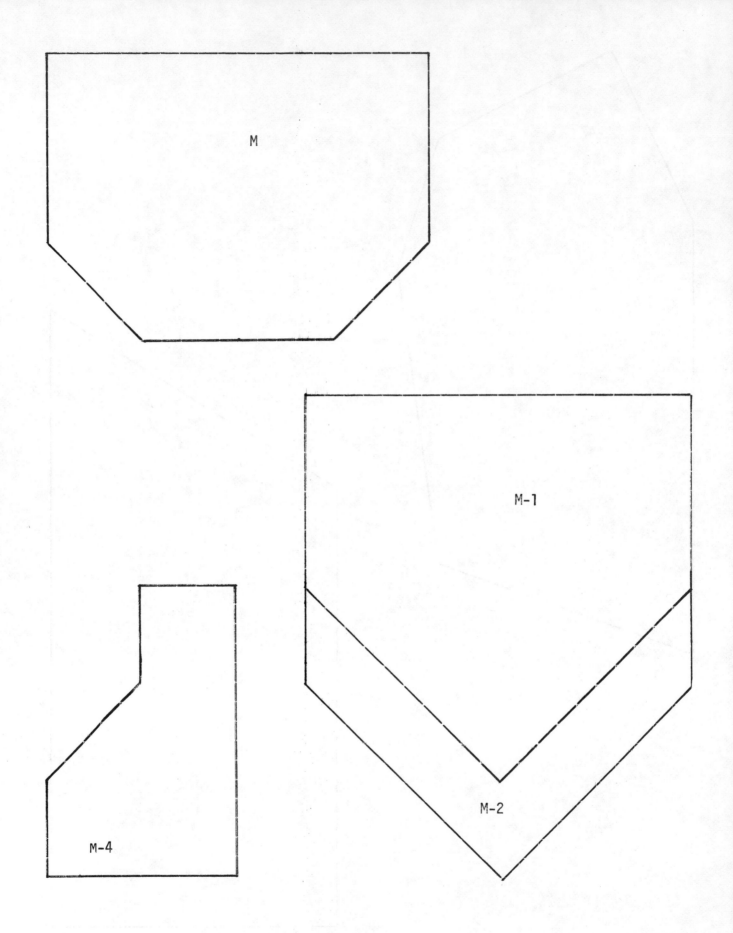

M

M-1

M-2

M-4

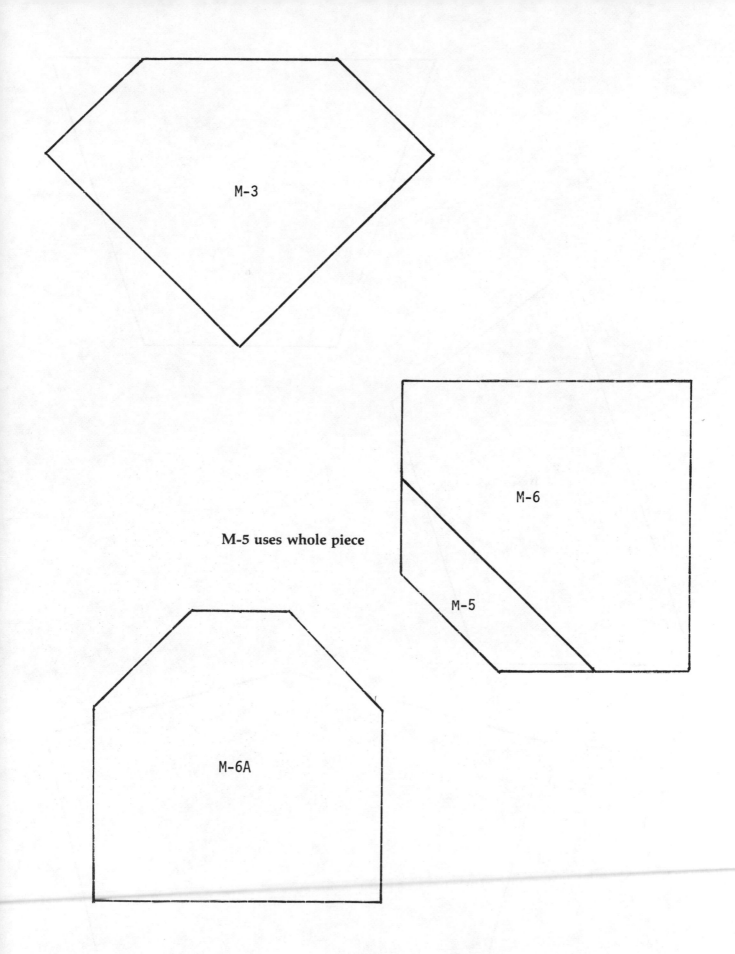

M-3

M-5 uses whole piece

M-6

M-5

M-6A

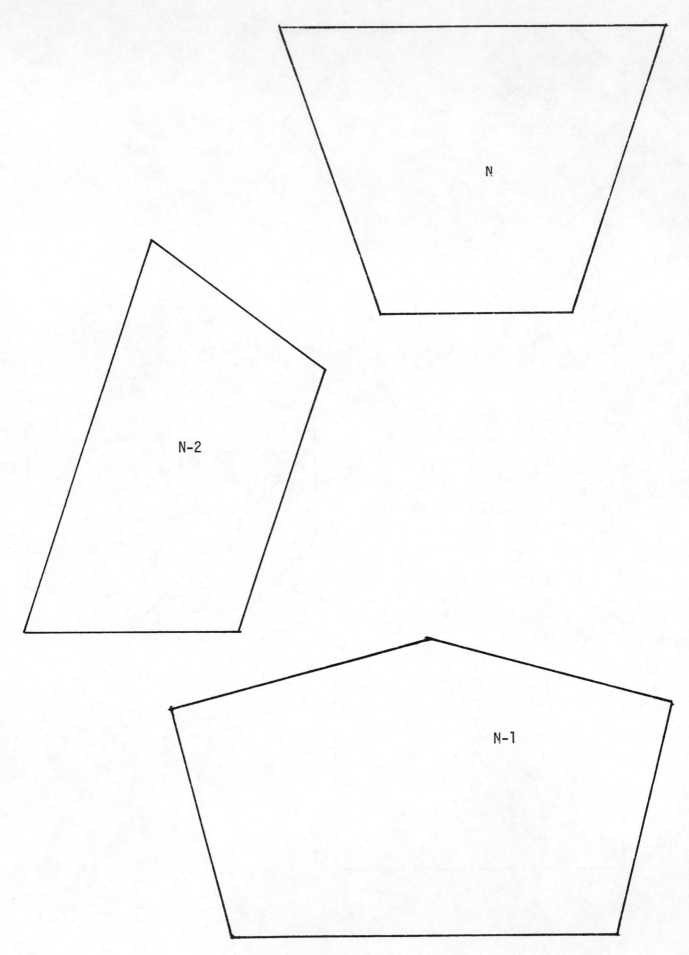

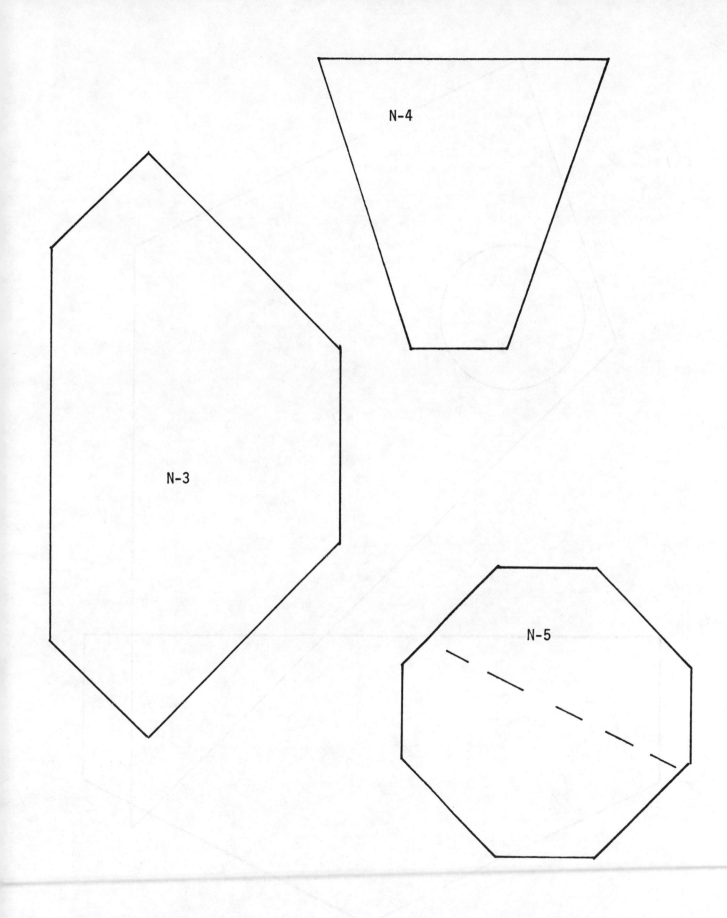

N-4

N-3

N-5

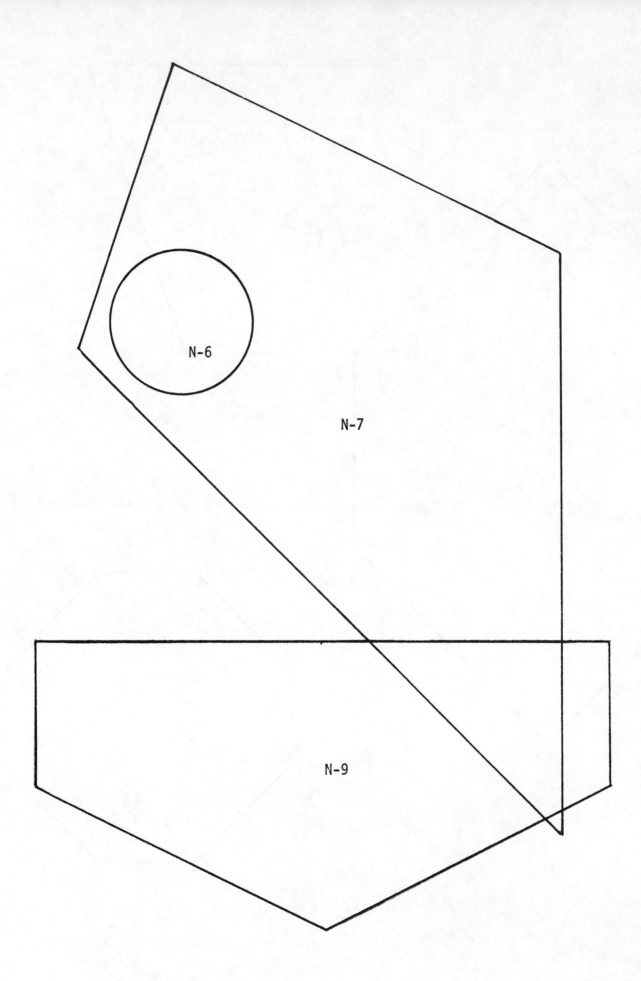

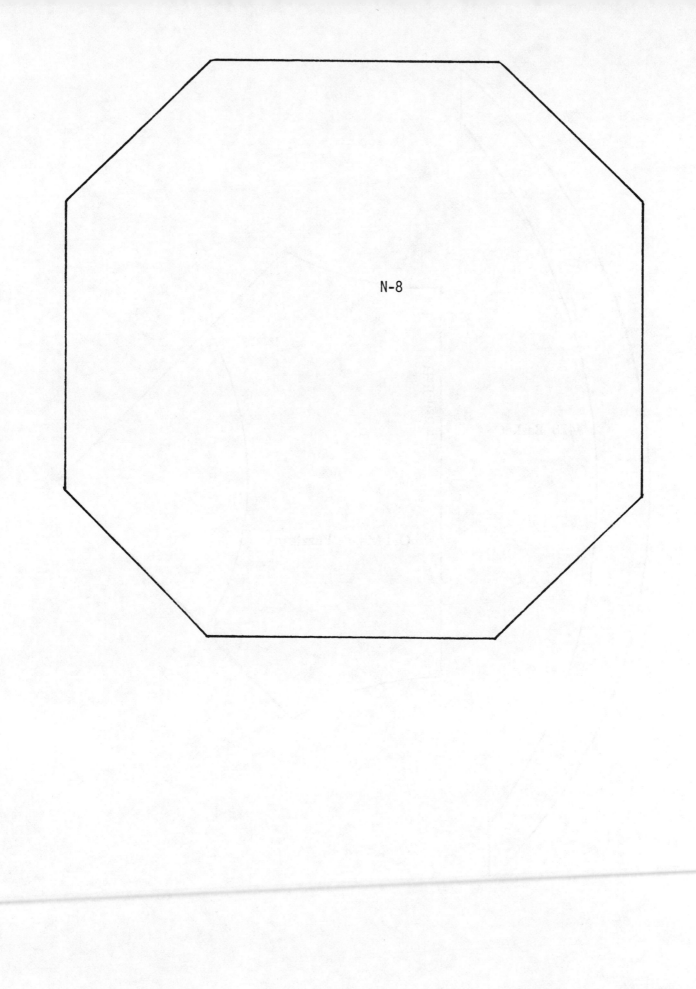

N-8

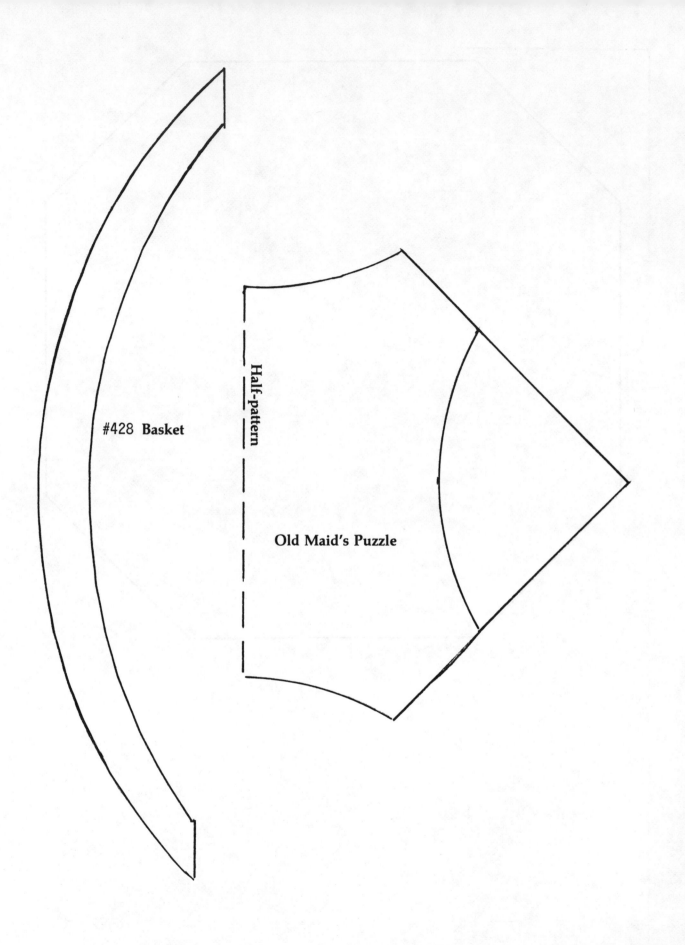

#428 Basket

Half-pattern

Old Maid's Puzzle

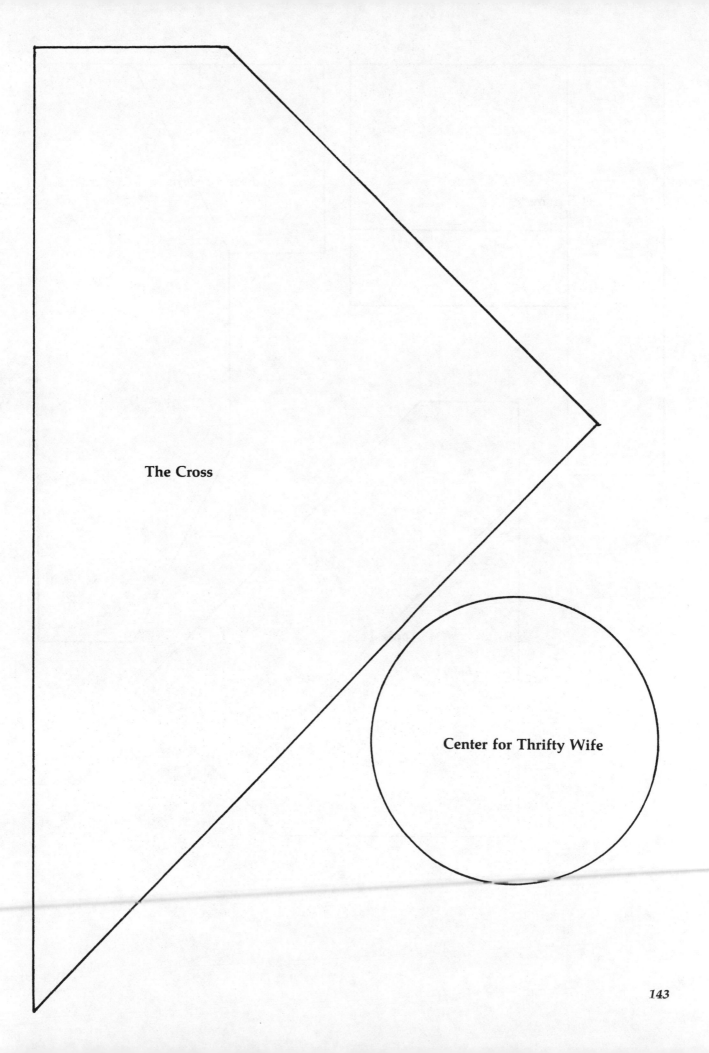

The Cross

Center for Thrifty Wife

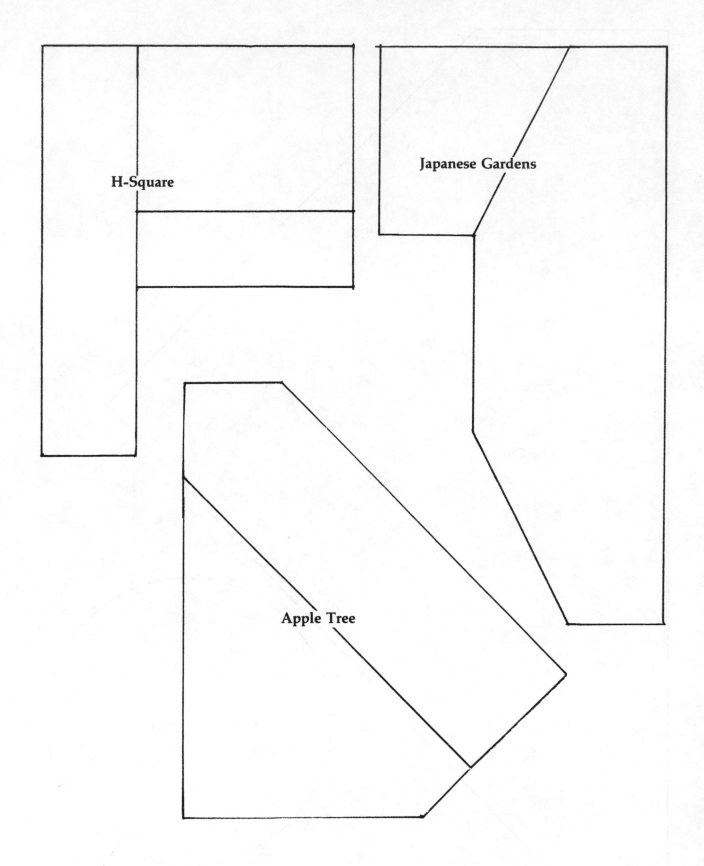

H-Square

Japanese Gardens

Apple Tree

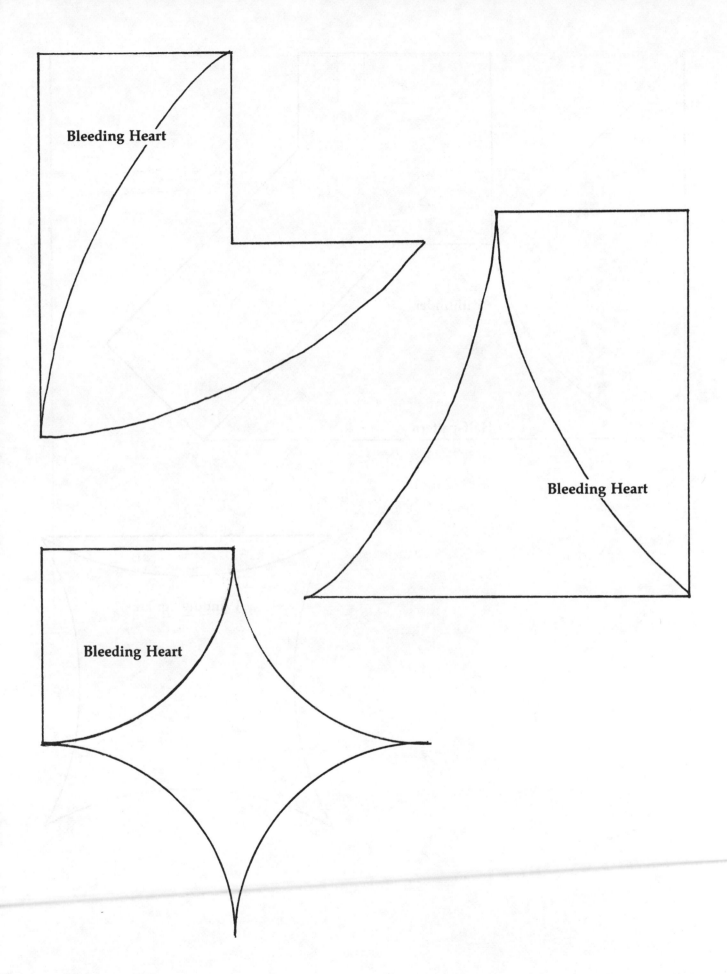

Bleeding Heart

Bleeding Heart

Bleeding Heart

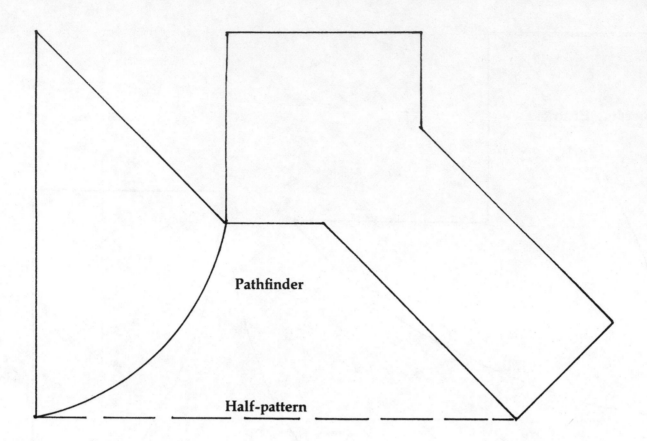

Pathfinder

Half-pattern

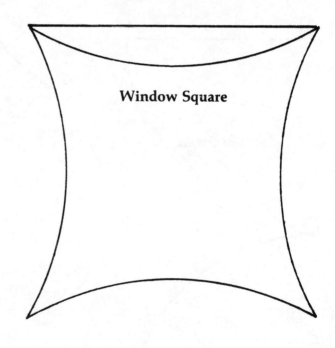

Window Square

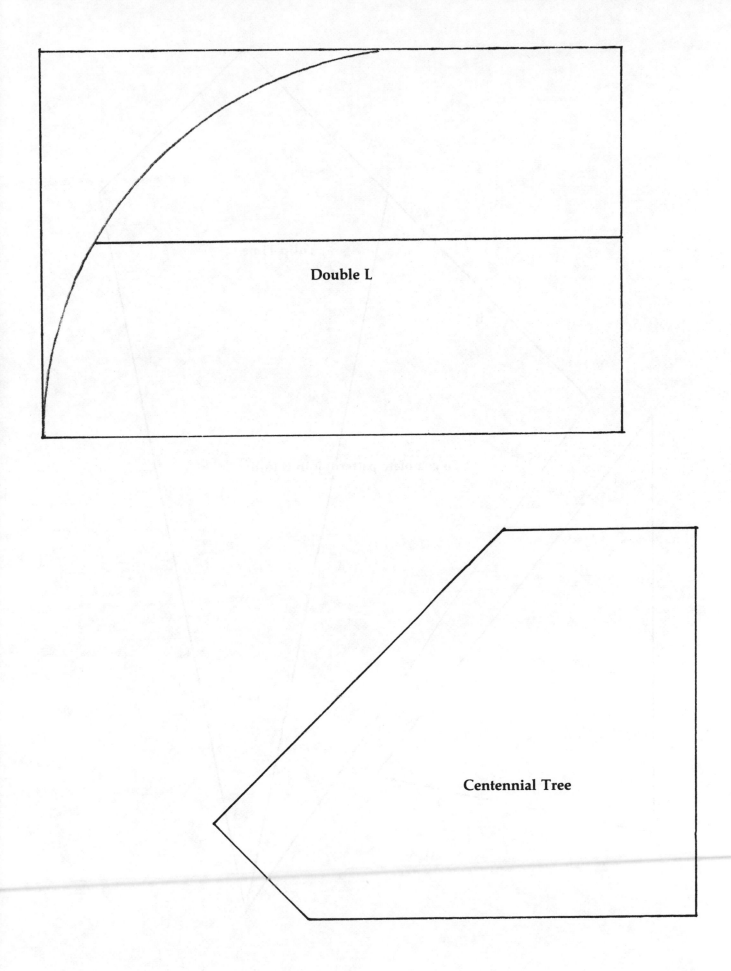

Double L

Centennial Tree

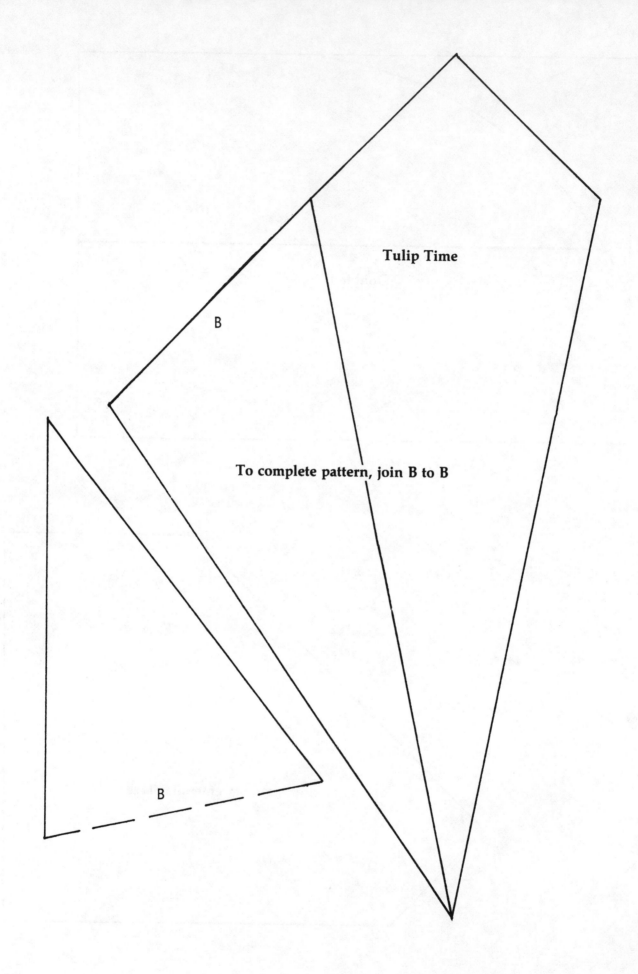

Tulip Time

To complete pattern, join B to B

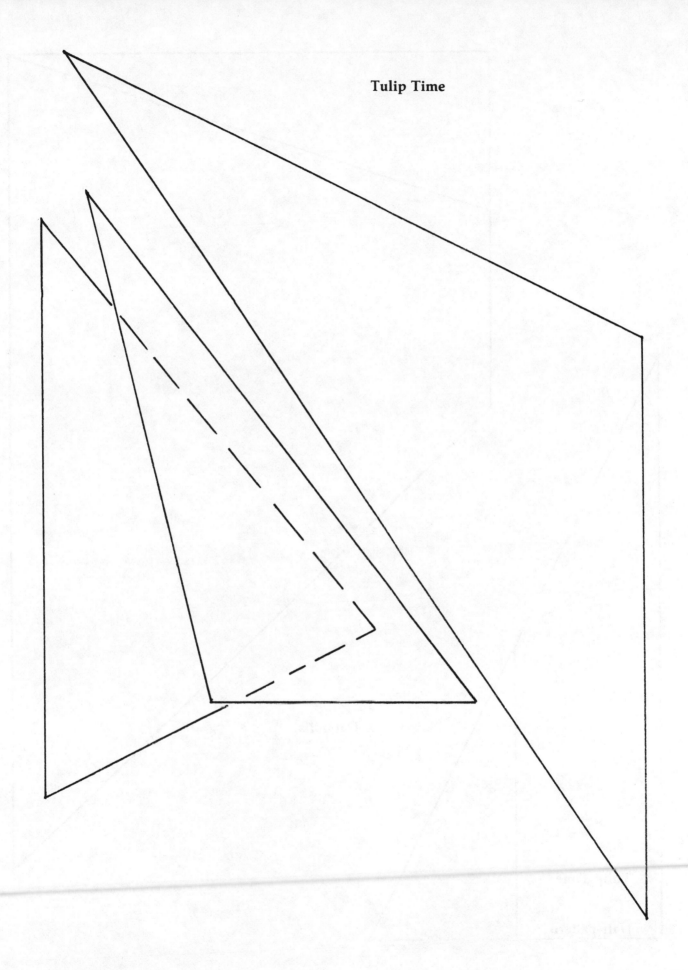

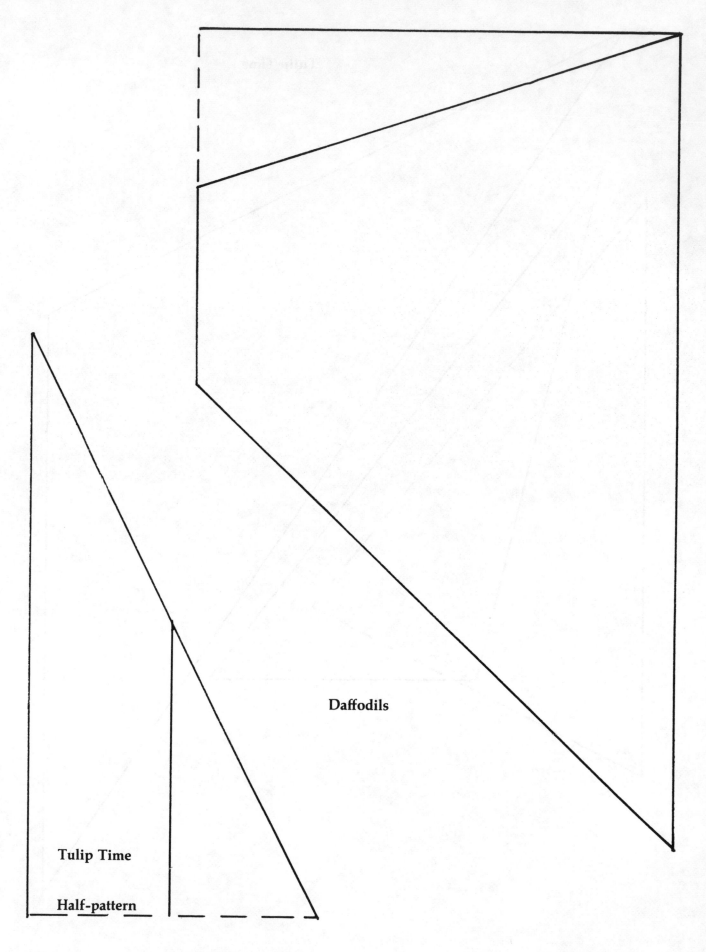

Daffodils

Tulip Time

Half-pattern

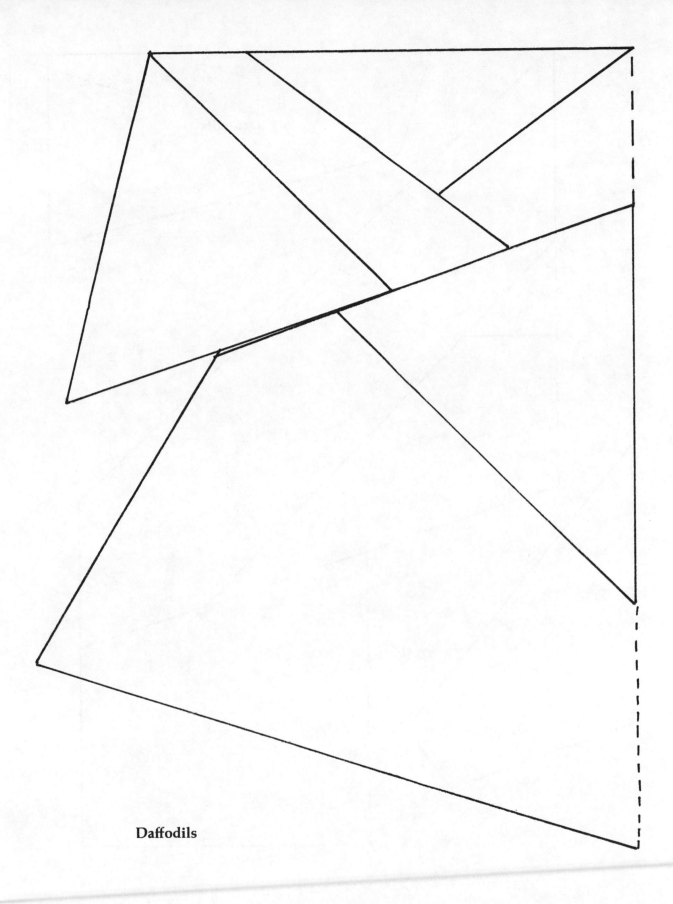

Daffodils

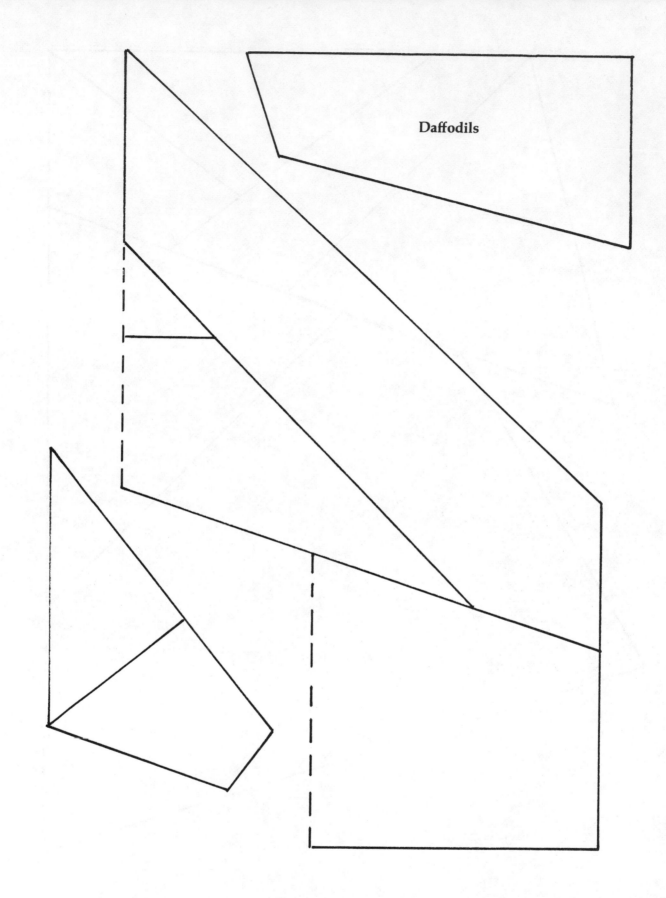

Daffodils

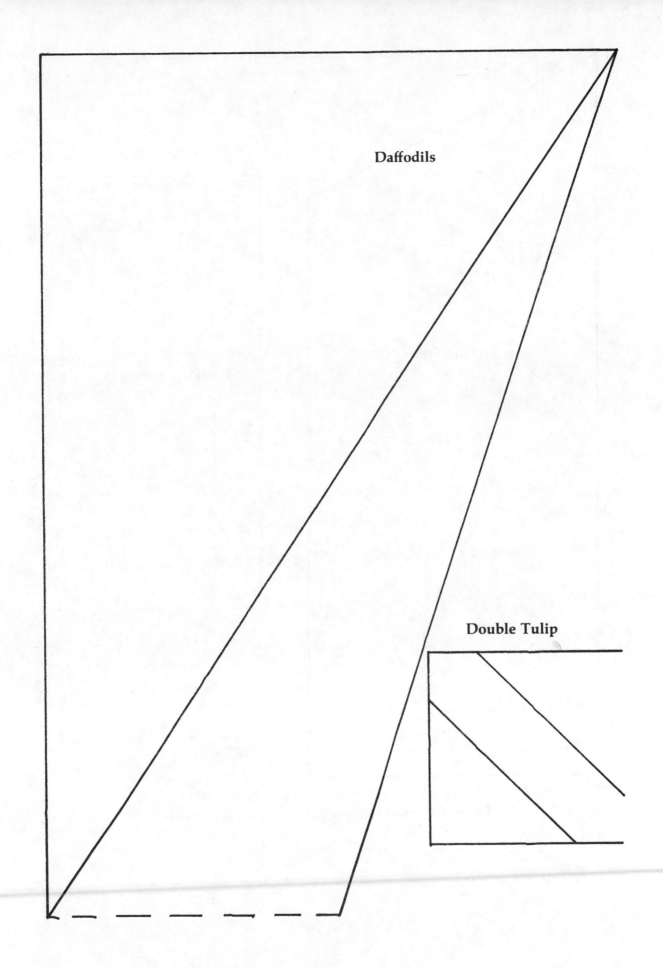

Daffodils

Double Tulip

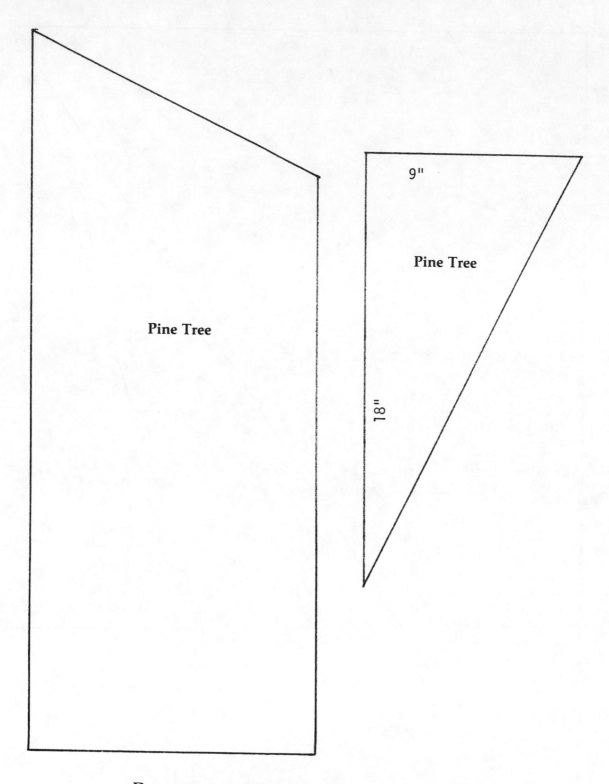

Pine Tree

9"

Pine Tree

18"

Draw pattern to full size for Pine Tree side pieces

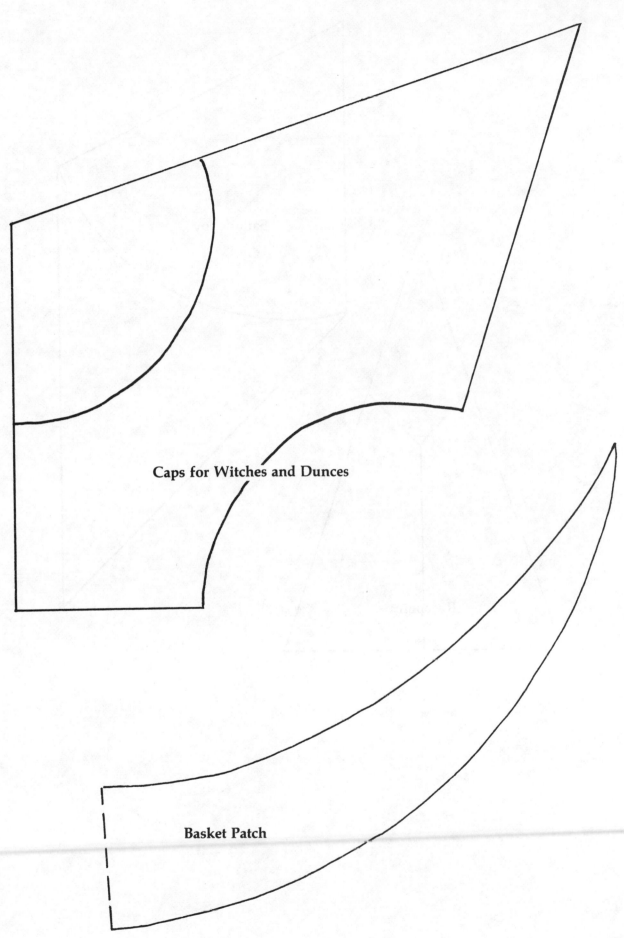

Caps for Witches and Dunces

Basket Patch

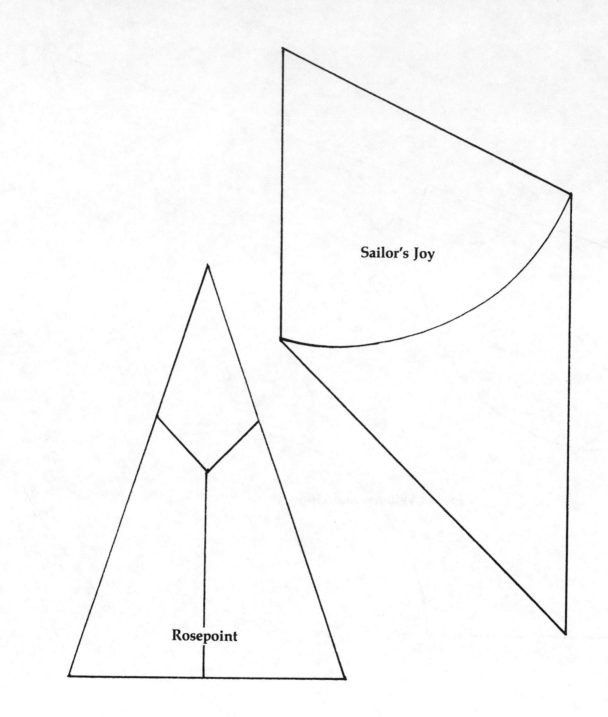

Sailor's Joy

Rosepoint

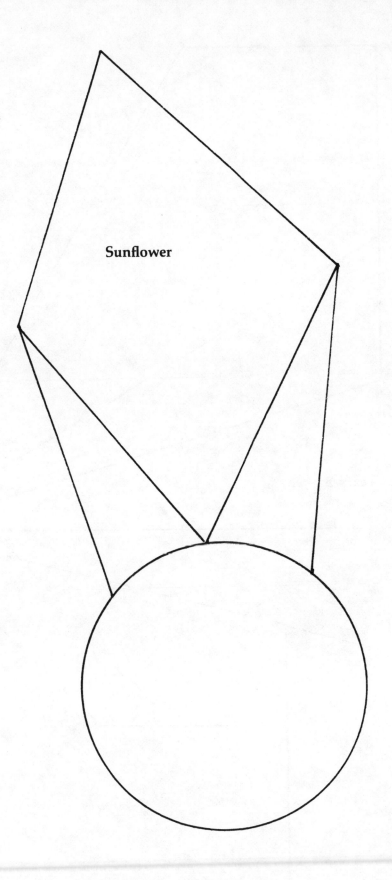

Sunflower

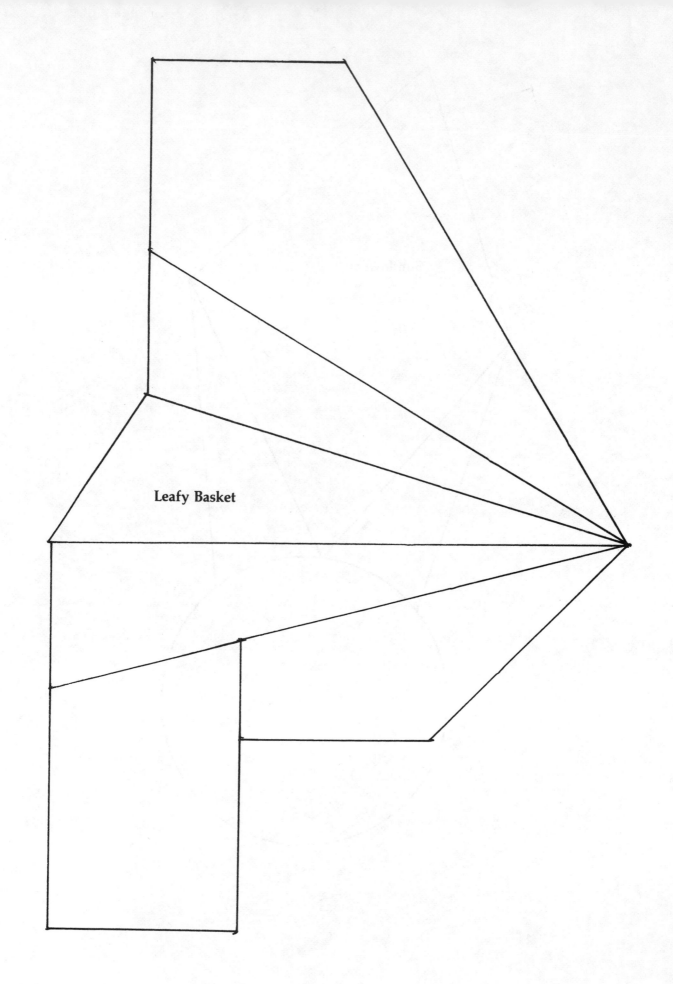

Leafy Basket

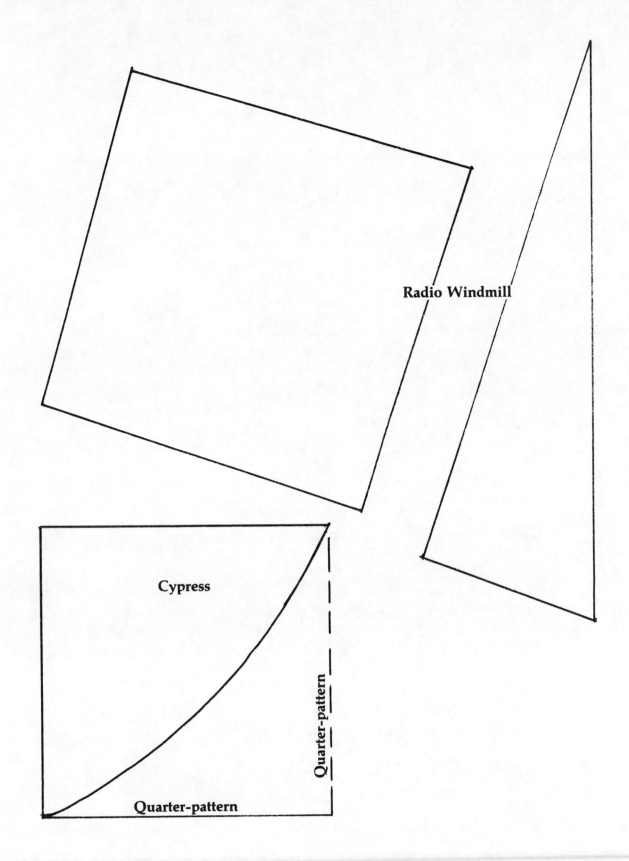

Radio Windmill

Cypress

Quarter-pattern

Quarter-pattern

APPENDICES

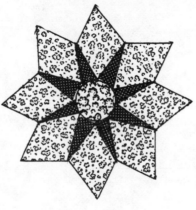

Estimating Yardage

After you have decided how large you want the quilt, it's time to determine what size block you will use. You should be flexible in this area, because block size and finished quilt size usually will not come out even. The following charts illustrate the problems that arise in arriving at an approximate quilt size of 78" × 106":

Block Size	Blocks Across	Blocks Down	Total Blocks Needed
8"	8 = 64"	10 = 80"	80
	9 2" strips = 18"	11 2" strips = 22"	

Finished Size: 82" × 102"

9"	7 = 63"	9 = 81"	63
	8 2" strips = 16"	10 2" strips = 20"	

Finished Size: 79" × 101"

10"	6 = 60"	8 = 80"	48
	7 3" strips = 21"	9 3" strips = 27"	

Finished Size: 81" × 107"

12"	5 = 60"	7 = 84"	35
	6 3" strips = 18"	8 3" strips = 24"	

Finished Size: 78" × 108"

14"	4 = 56"	6 = 84"	24
	5 3" strips = 15"	7 3" strips = 21"	

Finished Size: 71" × 105"
(This size may be better if set solid.)

15"	4 = 60"	5 = 75"	20
	5 3" strips = 15"	6 3" strips = 18"	

Finished Size 75" × 93"

If the lattice strips are made 4" wide:

	5 4" strips = 20"	6 4" strips = 24"	

Finished Size: 80" × 99"

16"	4 = 64"	5 = 80"	20
	5 4" strips = 20"	6 4" strips = 24"	

Finished Size: 84" × 104"

18"	3 = 54"	4 = 72"	12
	4 4" strips = 16"	5 4" strips = 20"	

Finished Size: 70" × 92"

Once the number of blocks needed for the quilt top has been determined you are ready to estimate how much fabric you need. I'll use a pattern that has been scaled to a 12″ block as an example.

Step 1: Determine total number of units per block: 4 white squares, 1 colored square, 4 white triangles, 4 colored triangles

Step 2: Multiply by total number of blocks:

4 × 48 = 192 white squares
192 colored triangles
192 white triangles
48 colored squares

Step 3: Add seam allowances to each of the units needed. Measure width and length of each of these units.

Step 4: Find the unit width on the accompanying chart. Go across to the second column to find how many units can be cut across the width of the fabric: 4″ square plus ½″ seam allowance = 5″ square = 9 units across fabric

Step 5: Find the unit length on the chart and follow it across to the third column to see how many units can be cut from the length of the fabric:

4″ square plus ½″ seam allowance = 5″ square = 7 units down fabric

Step 6: Multiply the number of units obtained in width by the number of units obtained in length to determine how many units can be cut from 1 yard of fabric: 9 units across × 7 units down = 63 per yard

Step 7: Divide total number of units needed by number of units per yard to obtain total yardage required: 192 divided by 63 = 3.04 yards. Repeat for each unit of block.

Unit Size	Number of Units Across (45″ fabric)	Number of Units Down (36″ fabric)
1″	45	36
1½″	30	24
2″	22	18
2½″	18	14
3″	15	12
3½	12	10
4″	11	9
4½″	10	8
5″	9	7
5½″	8	6
6″	7	6
6½″	6	5
7″	6	5
7½″	6	4
8″	5	4
8½″	5	4
9″	4	4

Quilt Index